S. 50
CaH

PRE-COLUMBIAN LITERATURES

A. ARIAS-LARRETA

Some other books by A. ARIAS-LARRETA

—*Radiografía de la Literatura Peruana*, 1945

—*Literaturas Aborígenes*, 1951-1962, (8 editions)

—*Rayuelo*, 1939-1963, (12 editions)

—*Incan Literature*, 1950

—*Nature and its Literary Expression*, 1952

—*Manual de Literatura Española*, 1954

—*Historia Crítica de la Literatura Indoamericana*, 1956

—*USA Educational Philosophy and Techniques*, 1958

PRE-COLUMBIAN LITERATURES

AZTEC - INCAN - MAYA-QUICHÉ

ABRAHAM ARIAS - LARRETA

Book I — History of Indoamerican Literature

"The Indians had and have the power for living which our modern world has lost — as world-view and self-view, as tradition and institution, as practical philosophy dominating their societies and as an art supreme among all the arts."

"As we traverse Indian history from the Conquest down to their present-day strivings, and up and down the two continents we come upon the Indian affirmative all through the record. For through all the slaughter of American Indian biological stocks, the slaughter of their societies and trampling upon their values, strange as it may seem, they have kept the faith. The inner-core value, complex and various, has not been killed. And since it has not been killed, it never will be. Be it for now or a hundred years from now, or a thousand — as long as the race of humanity shall survive — the Indians keep their gift as a gift for us all."

JOHN COLLIER

ACKNOWLEDGMENTS

The author wishes to thank the following institutions for their kind help and facilities rendered during his research work:

—Peruvian, Mexican, Guatemalan, British, French, and German National Museums.

—National Libraries of México, Perú, Guatemala, Bolivia, Madrid, Paris, Berlin, London, and Argentina; Library of Congress, Washington; Library of the Vatican, Rome; Archivo de Indias, Seville; Academy of History, Madrid; Museé de l'Homme, Paris; Newberry Library, Chicago; and libraries of the Universities of México and Guatemala.

PREFACE

RONALD HILTON *has the following words in his preface to Vasconcelo's* ULYSES:

> "The editor believes that the established hierarchy of values
> in Spanish literature are fossilized and conventional, and that
> if we judge Spain exclusively by its literature one is left with
> a quite distorted picture of what Spain is really like. The
> same goes for LATIN AMERICA, and, for that matter, for
> any country in the world."

*The words of professor Hilton, director of the Hispanic Institute
of Stanford University, are eloquent by themselves. We certainly need
a re-evaluation of Spanish and Spanish American literatures, and, in
addition, a re-tracing and an explanation of their literary process within
its own time and space patterns of historical relationships. Spanish
and Spanish American Literatures have been rarely comprehended in
this way, that is, as an organic whole. This fact is particularly noticeable in the histories of Spanish American literature, or* INDOAMERI-
CAN LITERATURE *as I used to call it, and I am going to call it
from now on.*

*During the 19th century the dominant theory of literary history
proposed that because "Spanish American literature was written in
Spanish," and because literature is expression and can presumably be
best described by the language in which it is expressed, "Spanish
American literature was, and always will be, a branch of Spanish
Literature." The fallacy is evident, but under its inspiration Indoamerican literature has been artificially divided, since 1800, into the
traditional periods of neo-clasicism, romanticism, realism, naturalism,
etc., in accordance with the western models of literary history.*

*A new theory of literary history appeared years later and pre-
tended to re-write our literary history according to rigid principles of
environment determinism. The theory and its school went so far in*

the search of records and documentation that the "artistic material" was hardly noticeable under the overwhelming burden of social and political data.

As a radical reaction against the determinist approach a group of literary historians took refuge in the aesthetic analysis, and tried to judge the literature as a timeless, spaceless, lifeless and "chemically pure" phenomenon.

Independently of the exclusivist theory followed in writing our literary history, most of the historians have incurred in a common failure—the complete exclusion of the initial chapter that corresponds to our pre-Columbian literatures. Our history, for them, apparently began, not five or ten thousand years ago, but only with the arrival of the Spanish conquerors. Some of those authors have advanced to deny the existence of an Indoamerican literature, by making use of a very curious reasoning—EUROPEAN CULTURE IS THE WESTERN CULTURE; SPANISH CULTURE IS EUROPEAN—SPANISH AMERICA IS ONLY A WESTERN CULTURAL COLONY.

As a result of these partial, incomplete and prejudiced approach the true history of Indoamerican literature has not yet been completely written. Many of the misunderstandings and prejudices have been cleared off, however, and the undeniable relationship between Indoamerican Literature and Indoamerican life has been definitely established. There is no reason why now a real history of Indoamerican literature can not begin to be written.

What can be termed as the "real history" of Indoamerican literature has been recently taking shape with some notable efforts made in the United States, in Mexico, Central and South America. But the complete and organic work is still waiting for a courageous writer, or for a qualified team of scholars like that who gave us the excellent ANTHOLOGY OF SPANISH AMERICAN LITERATURE—Herman Hespelt, John A. Crow, Irving Leonard, John Englekirk and John T. Reid.

As a modest contribution to the common cultural task I am publishing this book. Pre-Columbian Literatures is supposed to be the first chapter of any tentative history of Indoamerican Literature. According to my plans two more books will be published. The second volume is dedicated to the centuries in which our literature was mostly either a colonial branch of the so-called mother-country literature or a Spanish echo of European literature. The third volume is going to deal with the 19th and 20th centuries in a study that will follow the chronological succession of our literary generations instead of the classical order of the literary European schools. An organic view of history will guide me in establishing both—the cycles by which Indoamerican literature has been determined, and the high expressions of its aesthetic experiences through the most representative authors. Emphasis will be placed upon the contributions in finding and affirm-

ing an original literary expression for Indoamerica.

It seems unnecessary to insist, this time, in the value an importance of Pre-Columbian literatures. They are obvious. And the understanding of both, value and importance, is already evident, and also demonstrable by the growing interest in the study of the aboriginal literatures of America. Only by the existence of that understanding can be explained the warm welcome given to the eight editions of my LITERATURAS ABORIGENES.

The reader must know that this new book has only few things from my book in Spanish on the same subject. PRE-COLUMBIAN LITERATURES is, in fact, a new book in which I condensed the findings of many years of research and study. What has not changed is the double purpose of the book. It is the same as it was expressed in 1951: (1) To reveal the great literary message of the ancient civilizations of America, and (2) To reivindicate the rights of the pre-Columbian literatures in the history of Indoamerican literature.

ABRAHAM ARIAS-LARRETA

Mississippi State University

State College, Mississippi

TABLE OF CONTENTS

I

HISTORICAL

REFERENCES

The last word has not yet been said about the origin of "homus americanus."

According to the backers of the immigrationist theory, man reached our hemisphere, arriving from Asia, at the end of the Pliocene Period, across the Behring Strait or the Aleutian Islands, crossing the Pacific by the northern route from Polynesia, or crossing it directly from Australia. During the Pleistocene Period communication with Asia would have been interrupted and during the long isolation the race of the original inhabitants would have evolved with new types. At the end of the Pleistocene Period, the Asiatic immigrations were renewed, and cross-breeding with the natives would have produced a breed in whose features predominated a trace of the type evolved in our lands.

The autochthonists deny the first part of the immigrationist thesis. They contend that man was originally from our hemisphere, and endured all the vicissitudes of evolution, as did his other contemporaries in other parts of the world. They admit, however, the hypothesis of the later Asiatic immigrations, with people from the Paleolithic Age, and the consequent appearance of a new race as a result of the cross-breeding with the aborigines. There are authors who affirm that before these primitive immigrants, civilizations already existed, like the remotest Tiahuanacu, contemporaneous with Atlantis, long before the raising of the Andes, when the South American continent did not have as yet a definite shape.

The exponents of the two hypotheses agree, however, on one fact: the Stone Age immigrants were fishermen or hunters, perhaps they brought fire and some form of language, but all the vast development of agriculture occurred later, and the series of languages found by the Spaniards, were of indigenous creation, because linguistic studies have not traced any relationship between the Asiatic tongues and the indigenous American languages. No matter what may have been the origin of the American man, we can consider the Pre-Columbian cultures as "their own land's offspring", inasmuch as its elaboration was the undertaking of our first inhabitants in open fight with nature, forged in the perfect isolation in which they lived until the arrival of the Spanish Invaders.[1]

If the American is not autochthonous, then "he arrived into this world with simple knowledge and techniques peculiar to the Paleolithic Age. His later achievements he owes to himself, to his inventive genius which allowed him, little by little, to raise by his own means, a solid and original monument."[2] "The American man evolved from a stage of man as an animal, to the superior stage of man as a creator and director of cultures, without any discernible foreign influence".[3]

The forging of those cultures makes one think of the course of thousands of years. The same Louis Boudin believes that the American

3

men's antiquity is enormous if we take into consideration the centuries of culture represented by the use of the potato, the cultivation of corn, and the taming of cattle.[4] The arrival of man in the New World dates back more than 20,000 years, as held by Professor Erick Thompson.[5] Count Keyserling speculates that the formation of cultures in the Andine plateaus, over 10,000 feet high, originates from civilizations who searched for refuge in the high grounds, in remote centuries, fleeing from cataclysms and immemorial deluges.[6]

From what has been scientifically determined by Carbon-14 tests, the following calculations have been fixed for some American archaeological fossils:

9,000 years BC	Wendover, Utah, Danger Cave.
7 to 8,000 years BC	Nevada Gypsum Cave.
7,000 years BC	Lubbock Cave — Folson Culture.
9,000 years BC	Randolph County, Ill. Rock Ceiling.
9,000 years BC	Tepexpan Man. (Mexico)
5,000 years BC	Mexican agricultural cultures.

Carbon-14 tests are not yet extensive enough to determine the age of the archaeological findings. The antiquity of the American cultures seems to go back much more than 10,000 years before the Christian Era. It is also possible to surmise that during the time of aboriginal pre-history and proto-history, there may have existed an era of cosmopolitan civilizations, as complete and extensive as the one that has lived in the world since the discovery of America by the Europeans. We know practically nothing about that remote era, and very little knowledge has been attained, relatively, about the later indigenous history. What can be stated, without controversy, is that upon Columbus' arrival there lived in our continent numerous organized societies, on a different level of progress, but with their own culture and autonomous evolution, and that many other civilizations had preceded them, because their existence was registered in narrative and legend, and was fully attested by the presence of many monuments.

A Pre-Columbian map, immediately prior to the Spanish invasion, would show us the following aboriginal societies: Esquimos (North Pole, Alaska); Redskins (United States of North America); Aztecas, Tecpanecas, Chichimecas, Tlacastecas (Mexico); Quiches, Cakchiqueles (Guatemala); Pipiles (El Salvador); peoples of Maya origin (Copan-Honduras); Nahoas of Chinatlan, Nagradanos, Chorotegas (Nicaragua); Borucas (Costa Rica); Caribes, Siboneyes, Borinqueños (Antilles); Chibchas (Colombia); Cañaris (Ecuador); Yungas (Peruvian Coast); quechuas, collas, aymaras (Peruvian and Bolivian Andes); Araucanos and Atacamas (Chile); Guaranies (Brazilian, Paraguayan and Argentinian Zones). Calchaquiés (Tucuman, Santiago del Estero);

4

Charrúas (Uruguay); Fueguinos and Patagonians (southern zones of Chile and Argentina).

The so-called high cultures inhabited, approximately, the areas that today correspond to (1) the central and meridional parts of Mexico; (2) part of the Mexican South and West, Guatemala, Honduras, Nicaragua, El Salvador; (3) the present territory of Perú, Bolivia, Ecuador, Chile, and part of Colombia and Argentina. These areas were occupied, respectively, by the Aztec, Maya, Maya-Quiché and Incan cultures. At the time of the Spanish invasion, the second Mayan empire was already extinct; the conquerors found only their descendants (Quiché Kingdom, Capital: Utatlán; Cakchiquel Kingdom, Capital: Ixinché; the kingdom of the Zutugiles, Capital: Atitlán; the kingdom of the Pipiles, Capital: Cuxcatlán, among others) and the imposing ruins that run from Copán to Chichen-Itzá.

According to the conclusions reached by the Fifth Round Table of the Mexican Anthropological Society (Jalapa, Veracruz, 1951) the picture of the Mexican Pre-Columbian cultures can be summarized this way: a) The existence of a basic culture, along the length of the Gulf of Mexico, which corresponds to a substratum of Mayan-speaking peoples, which constitutes the oldest archaeological horizon; b) This original culture is divided into two branches: the one of Remojadas, in the center, which later extends to the Valley of Mexico, and develops until the blooming of the Teotihuacana or Toltec culture, and the Olmecan, to the south of the Gulf coast, which extends itself in the so-called Classical Mayan culture. These cultures emigrate from the Gulf coast in opposite directions and evolve independently; c) Two types of culture from different sources unite in the central part of Mexico; d) There is an abrupt change in the archaeological panorama which corresponds to the admission of the Toltec horizon into Guatemala and Yucatan, superimposing itself on the Mayan; e) The high cultures of the central region of Mexico, proceeding from the south, advance towards the altiplano or across the Gulf; f) After the Toltecan collapse, they return to their native countries.

THE MAYAN CULTURE

Max Uhle has held that the Mayas were the forerunners of the South-American civilizations. His theory has been firmly supported by Rafael Girard, for whom the Mayan-Toltecan civilization is born and developed in the Mayan zone of the Pacific, which zone is to this continent what the Tigris and Euphrates zones were to the Old World, that is, the matrix of its cultures. A Mexican writer, Humberto Magaloni, when questioned as to what is called Mayan culture, goes further with this answer: "It would be better to say Indian culture, because all the nations of this continent shared it: the Mayas, the Teotihuacanos, the Nahuatls, the Quichés, the Quechuas".[7] Developing a bold and novel theory, Magaloni goes on to say that the Mayas were the instructors of the Egyptians in the construction of the pyramids, and that in every world language there are Mayan roots. "World culture was born in our continent," he affirms.

The original thesis has been devaluated somewhat—insofar as it concerns the Mayan progeniture of the South American civilizations—due to the discovery in the amazonic regions of a culture as advanced as that of the Incas,[8] and is contradicted by the authors who support the existence of an original Colla nucleus, the center of the South American cultural irradiation (Diez de Medina, Arturo Posnansky).[9]

The origin of the Mayas, as well as that of the Collas and Aymaras (the legendarian Antis of the Perú-Bolivian highland plain), has not yet been well determined. What has been already incorporated as an historical truth is the existence of a first Mayan empire between

6

Guatemala, Honduras and the Mexican States of Chiapas and Tabasco, with an apogee and decadence between the years 639 and 899 BC, and a second Mayan empire, or a renaissance, with principal centers in Chichen-Itzá, Mayapán and Uxmal, which started to fall around the year 1437 AD approximately.

In order to appreciate the splendid development of the Mayan culture it suffices to remember the expressions of its artistic potency in sculpture and drawings; the complete mastery of the astronomical science (its calendar proved to be better than the Spaniards' and rivals the Gregorian in exactness); the creation of a writing with a graphic representation of its phonemes, the discovery of the position of the numbers and the use of the zero prior to the Hindus; the admirable development of the pictorial art (The Palace of the Tigers in Chichen-Itzá), the conception of the Popol-Vuh and other documents of great literary value; their surprising architectural skill, and the wondrous level of its philosophical speculations, which led them to the supreme conception of the universe, surmising, many centuries before Einstein, that matter is a concentration of energy, and going beyond Einstein, as Magaloni reminds us, in thinking that "from energy to spirit there is only one step".

THE MAYA-QUICHÉS

The Quichés, whose descendants still inhabit Guatemala, possess, like the Cakchiqueles, a definite Mayan ancestry. From this ancestry we get the name Maya-Quiché, for the culture they built; although, according to historical facts, that designation would properly correspond to the initial period of their history, and not to the following periods (that of the separation of the Mayas; that of the formation of a culture in the Tula or Tulán region (Central Mexico) in contact with the Nahuas (Toltecan culture); that of their return to Guatemala, their country of origin, together with groups of Cakchiqueles and Yaquis to displace the archaic Mayas, and finally, that of the independent evolution of the Quiché culture in whose aspects were accentuated the profiles created in Mexico, differing it from the renascent Mayan culture, which continues with its old momentum, but in different direction).

The exodus of the Quichés and their followers began, according to approximate calculations, in the Seventh Century of the Christian Era. It left from Tula, after the Toltec collapse, and coincided with that of the founders of Uxmal and Chichen-Itzá in the Yucatan peninsula. According to Morley[10] the group of the Ah-Atzaes was the one that, years later, established itself in Chichen-Itzá. It was probably the Itzá tribe that lived 250 years in Campeche, having come from the South, bringing the culture of the old Mayan empire, and the one that, according to the Chilam Balam of Chumayel, proceeded from

7

the hill of Kanek, the name of the chief of Peten-Itzá or the Land of the Nine Hills (a region situated on the shores of the Chixoy River, a tributary of the historic Usumacinta). Before or after the Ah-Itzaes, would have arrived Kukulcán (the Toltec Quetzalcoatl), who taught the arts and sciences and was founder of Mayapán. At the same time the founding of Uxmal would have been carried out by Tutul Xiú and his companions coming from Tulapan.

When the Quiché kingdom had as its capital the opulent city of Gumarcaah or Utatlán, their conquests had stretched to the mountains of the Nabes, the Pacific Coast from Soconusco, the limits of Petén and the territory of the Cakchiqueles and Zutujiles. The Quiché dynasty began the year 1054 and succeeded itself in the government without interruption for 480 years. During that time 14 sovereigns governed the Quiché nation, according to the Popol Vuh.

The following are the characteristics that distinguish the Fourth Age of the Quiché history:

— Patriarchal-agrarian Cycle: Social preponderance of man, suppression of human sacrifices; theocratic government, agriculture based on the cultivation of corn and ruled by an agrarian code.

— Religious spiritualism, high level ethics, baptism with water.

— Advanced architecture and sculpture. Masculine idols, echeloned pyramid, monumental patios for ball games, stone thrones.

— Creation of the Maya-Quiché theater. Use of the "boronte" (a drink out of corn and cacao).

— Moon-Sun Calendar: the Tzolkin, corn calendar; the Tun (36 days) for the climate and seasons of Guatemala; the Haab (365 days and cycle of 52 years). This original calendar, as affirmed by Girard, is an exclusive creation of the Maya-Quiché culture, without parallel among the chronological systems of antiquity, as it adjusts all the activities of the life of the community and the individual to the universal rhythm.

THE AZTECS

The Toltecan collapse already mentioned determined the exodus of the human groups that forged its culture. According to Clavigero[11] these are the approximate dates of the principal events in the history of Central Mexico:

Arrival of the Toltecs to the Anahuac Plateau	648 BC
Toltecan collapse	1051 AD
Arrival of the Chichimecas	1170 AD
Arrival of the Alcohua	1200 AD
Entry of the Mexicans in Tula	1196 AD
Founding of Mexico	1325 AD

After the fall of Tollan Teotihuacán (Tula or Tulán for other authors), and before the arrival of the Mexicans to the plateau, there flourished the so-called intermediate cultures that can be represented by the Tarascos of Michoacan and the Mixteco-Zapotecas of Oaxaca. From the latter remain the impressive ruins of Mitla and the archaeological remains of Monte Alban.

Many peoples already existed and warred among themselves when the Aztecs, the future Mexicans, commanded by Tenoch and led by the God Huitzilopochtli, ended their long pilgrimage from the legendary Aztlan region, over the plateau of Anahuac. They were the Alcohuanos, Chichimecas, Tlacatecas, Tecpanecas, Tlaxcalas. After founding their capital, the sacred city of Tenochtitlan, the Aztecs organized, disciplined and hardened an army, and began to intervene actively in the political and military life of the plateau. The most sagacious act during this period was the alliance with Netzahualcoyotl, the Alcohuan king, to whom they returned the control of his kingdom after defeating his enemies, the Tecpanecas. By that time Texcoco, the Alcohuan capital, had surpassed the other important capitals like Tenayuca and Atzcapotzalco, while Tenochtitlan was still a shack town. The Aztecs had already become the arbiters of the situation, however, due to their military might. The political center of power, and later that of culture were slowly transferred from Texcoco to Tenochtitlan, the city of the lakes.

About the year 1500, having as a center the Anahuac Valley, a powerful confederation had been formed on the basis of the Aztecs of Tenochtitlan, the Alcohuas of Texcoco, and the settlers of the kingdom of Taclopan. The confederation governed practically all the actual territory of Mexico, and within it the Aztecs held predominant rank, reserving for themselves the military command.

According to the chroniclers of the Indies, the military power was in the hands of the *Tlacatecuhtli*, a lifetime post, but not hereditary, and the civil power was held by the *Cihuacohuatl*. Over these chiefs was the *Tlatocan*, a sort of Supreme Council, formed by the representatives of the confederate peoples.

At one time, shortly after the arrival of the Aztecs, each family received a plot of land for their permanent usufruct. If the family became extinct, or the land was not cultivated within a determined time limit, the plot returned to the *calpulli*, or community, to be newly distributed among the neediest. The nobility and the temples were the only possessors of private wealth. This communal regime of the land disappeared as a type of feudal system of property started to take hold. The incipient feudalism, in violent contrast with the traditional system, had its origin in the distribution of land made by Otzcoatl, a Technoca king, conqueror of the Tecpanecas. The then leader of the confederation distributed among individuals the lands seized from the vanquished. In this manner the heroes of the war against the enemies

9

of Netzahualcoyotl were the first owners of private property and became, in time, real feudal barons. The caste system, then inaugurated, went on consolidating and increasing its powers until the elimination of the ancient communal regime of land ownership and the democratic forms of social and political organization which that regime upheld. The feuds grew rapidly at the expense of the lands of the calpulli and servitude showed its face, a new and odious institution. Years later there existed great masses of indigents, dispossessed persons and malcontents, in whose breasts brewed a dreadful rebellion, ready to explode, according to some authors, about the time of the beginning of the Spanish invasion.

Before that sorry state of affairs, life among the Aztecs had surprisingly democratic characteristics. There were certain temporal forms of slavery by the war of conquest, but nobody was born a slave. The social cell was the exogamous clan, the union of the clans formed the tribe and this, in turn, was governed by a council with proportional representations from all the clans. The tribal functionaries, as well as the chiefs of the clan, were elected on merit, and not for any other consideration. In this way a democratic system of government was established in which there was rank, but not interests of caste or oligarchial privileges.

In the Aztec religion, above all the idols and gods, existed the Supreme God, the One Cause, *Ometecuhtli*. Second in hierarchy was *Quetzalcoatl*, the beneficent god, master of sciences, arts and industry. *Huitzilopochtli*, god of war, was the deity who could not nourish himself except with life, "the magic substance that is found in man's blood". The Aztecs offered him human sacrifices (like the ancestors of the Greeks, the Teutons and the Celts and with other purpose than that of the "Holy Inquisition, with its 'burnings' "). I do not share the prejudicial words of Prescott about human sacrifices among the Aztecs. I agree, however, with the words of Collier,[12] who upon commenting on Spinden's pertinent concepts, says that the "victim" of those sacrifices did not consider himself a victim but rather some sort of fortunate hero, who advanced in ecstasy to the sacrifice, believing himself chosen, and firmly believing that his transfiguration, after death, was made for the benefit of the world and his race.

The Aztecs conducted commerce actively with numbers, measures, and a substitute for metal money. From their ancestors they inherited the monumental architecture, the science of astronomy, the art of paper manufacture and progress in painting and sculpture. They knew writing and perfected an original system of education. The splendid literature they have bestowed us in the Nahuatl tongue is, even today, the most complete among the aboriginal civilizations. Paul Morand declared that its prodigious sculptures arrived at the simplification of planes and volumes searched for much later by modern artists (the head of the Knight of the Eagle surprised the celebrated Rodin be-

10

cause of its expressive power). In the decorative art they matched the most refined civilizations.

Only now is the art of the Pre-Columbian civilizations starting to be considered in its exact meaning. Historians and critics—leaving the dogmatic tradition of occidental art—are beginning to understand that the erroneously called aboriginal American "primitive art" is not an inferior art nor an inferior stage of art, but the culmination of a long and magnificent process of artistic creation. And there are critics who hold the opinion that such masters as Picasso and Modiglioni have created works which are inferior to the ones of the great indigenous sculptors.

Great though it was, and unequaled in many respects, the Aztec confederation had also its failures. The expansion of its dominions was due to war of conquest, and this did not bear a civilizing purpose nor did it try to achieve the organic assimilation of the vanquished peoples. Formed by heterogenous and warlike baronies, it did not have the solid unity of Empire of the Incas, for example. The most unfortunate of its historical failures was the admission of the feudal system. Upon breaking the magnificent communal foundations of the social-economic life, the democratic system irremediably began to fall. This fact, perhaps more than any other, favored the advance of the Spanish invaders in 1519.

Prescott is right when he affirms that the disintegration of the great confederation was the fault, in great part, of its own subjects. "Their fate can serve us as a pathetic proof that a government that does not rest on the support of the governed, cannot last, and that the social institutions, when not based on the progress and welfare of the people, must fall by the hand of violence, either internal or external".[13]

THE PRE-INCAN ERA

The empire of the Incas appears, viewed from an historical perspective, as the last stage of a cultural evolution, the first steps of which date back more than 10,000 years BC. The Spanish invaders found a mature and polished civilization with social institutions of organic functioning, master of a skillful and original art, in possession of evolved religious beliefs, taking pride in a welfare of a high order based on the benefits derived from an economic system scientifically planned, controlled and apportioned. The Incas could not have created all this in the few centuries assigned to them by history. They inherited, therefore, as is logically supposed, the most significant cultural conquests of the preceding civilizations, and set them to work in a dynamic, organic and functional system. They gave the historical contribution which concerned them, but their ingenious work was that of selecting and reorganizing the millenarian cultural heritage, and its accurate projection into the future. This renowned task could not be achieved without the possession of a defined historical conscience, without counting on a powerful systematizing genius, and without the existence of a philosophy to standardize the progress and fix the goals to be conquered in the development of the Inca civilization.

The Incas possessed that conscience, that genius and that philosophy. The cultural heritage over which they operated was bequeathed by the pre-Incan civilizations. Even today the studies and investigations do not dare to deal much with the proto-history, and have carried out only certain probes in the Incan pre-history. With the little that is known, the first thing that has been tried is a classification of the different cultures that preceded the Empire of Tahuantinsuyo. One of the clearest is the one formulated by the North American professor Wendell Bennett.[14] According to him there were six periods in the archaeological history of South America, including the Incan. The first period goes from 1200 to 400 BC and is represented by the Chavin Culture (there are fabrics, however, of an earlier antiquity than 3000 years BC according to Carbon-14 Tests). The second period (400 BC to 1000 AD) presents us to civilizations with a complete dominion of nature, an advanced social organization, extraordinary progress in architecture, sculpture, hydraulic engineering, goldsmithing, and ceramics. This period is represented by the civilizations of Mochica (with the most famous sculptors), Parakas (Pre-Incan weavers without peer) and Nazca (unequaled colored ceramics). The fourth period saw the coastal empire of the Great Chimú and the mountain empire of the Tiahuanacu. In the Chimú empire flourished a refined civilization of ceramists, weavers, goldsmiths, and farmers, heiress of the cultural conquests of the Mochicas. Its capital was the city of Chanchan, with an extension of eight square miles, with great pyramids, superb palaces, walls of finished adobe, magnificent gardens and enormous reservoirs of stone for irrigation. The empire of the Tiahuanacu that Bennett places in this period of 1000 to 1300 years AD, is, without doubt, the second empire, because it is believed that the first one existed 900 to 500 BC, and there are authors that date back the roots of the Tiahuanacan civilization many thousands of years before the Christian Era.

We shall never have a complete vision of the Pre-Incan civilizations until the great chapter of those civilizations, with roots differentially Colla, are fully investigated. Arturo Posnansky deduces from his investigations that the Collas possess one of the earliest antiquities among the peoples of the earth. Upon observing the descendants of the Collas in Bolivia, Count Keyserling exclaimed: "these men are much older than what has been supposed until today."[15] Fernando Diez de Medina holds that "the Inca Empire was not the primitive Andean Universal state, but the substitute of the prior empire of the Collas". And refuting Toynbee's theory that the coast precedes the mountain culturally, he affirms that "it is precisely the contrary. Chimú, Nazcan and the Incan (the latter inheriting something from the two cultures, the coastal and the Andean), derive from the great Andean or Collan central nucleus, of evident cordilleran roots. The Great Cordillera in its epic culmination at the Bolivian Andean plateau, is not only a geological event, it is the greatest and remotest habitat of the South American". Diez de Medina finishes this stating: "I remain with my vision of an Andean culture, the flower of many cultures, ancient, palingenesic, built, destroyed and rebuilt many times, and I accept only as its end the Inca civilization, which is only a minimum part of the prehistoric events which occurred in the great South American cordillera."[16] Arnold Toynbee, in a letter dated the 13th of July 1951, answered Diez de Medina, stating among other things: "I admit that my knowledge of Andean history are not very deep, and on account of that I am ready to believe that I do not carry enough weight to give the Colla the importance it has in the creation of the Andean civilizations."[17]

The idea is gaining ground that there was a master Andean civilization whose first steps date much further back than anything that has been deduced or imagined to date. There is no existing doubt about the Pre-Incan Tiahuanacu and its vast historical influence, inasmuch as the Aymara was the predominant language in the era prior to the Incas. The Ayllu, the long-lasting social cell of the Tahuantinsuyo, was a legacy of that powerful civilization, and its classical echeloned sign, as well as its lithic architecture, reminds us of the Collan claw in practically every one of the coastal and mountain civilizations. Its conquests must have gone and advanced to the four cardinal points, as is demonstrated by the toponymy in such remote places as Venezuela, and is repeatedly attested in the ceramics and textile works, the archaeological findings in Cuzco, Nazca, Pachacamac, Lurin, Huari, Charcas and those of the Chiriguanos, Atacameños, Araucanos and Chimús.

13

Of course the picture of the Pre-Incan civilizations of Professor Bennett is temporary and incomplete. We could say the same about the classification made by Rebeca Carrion Cachot, in which we miss some cultures like those of San Pedro, Ancon, Cupiznique, Chicama, Salinar, Recuay, Chancay, etc. But it is a more didactical classification than Bennett's, therefore it is worth knowing:

Archaic Era — 4 to 2000 years BC   Chavin-Huaylas-Pukara.

Intermediate Era — 2 to 1000 years BC   Tiahuanacu-Parakas-Kollawa.

Classical Era — 1000 years BC to 400 years AD   Chimú (1 Muchic, Nazca-Cuzco.

14

THE INCAS

The Empire of the Incas or of Tahuantinsuyo, appears with its first definite characteristics in the Eleventh Century. Thirteen sovereigns ruled the destinies of the empire as shown in the following chart:

Era of the Confederation (Hurincuzco Dynasty):

Manco Capac, founder of the Empire.

Sinchi Roca (the prudent warrior).

Lloque Yupanqui (the famous left-hander).

Mayta Capac (Great Lord).

Capac Yupanqui (valiant).

Hanancuzco Dynasty:

Inca Rocca (Prudent lord).

Yauar Huacca (he who weeps blood).

Unification of the Empire:

Huiracocha (water foam).

Pachacutec (the most powerful on earth).

Amaru Inca (Serpent Lord).

Tupac Inca Yupanqui (Memorable Lord).

Huayna Capac (Powerful Lord).

Huascar and Atahualpa.

Highly developed civilizations existed long before the Ayar brothers' pilgrimage from Tamputoco to found an Empire, by command of their father, the Sun, or urged by primary necessities. There flourished already the textile industry among the Parakas with their austere chromatic tonalities; there lived the Nazcans, ceramists without peer, who discovered a way to vanquish the dryness of their land with the ingenious terraced pathway of the spiral, the Chimús were there, who had achieved marvels of finished adobe and prodigious works of hydraulic engineering. The Mochicans had already passed on, whose amazing sculptural ability has no parallel in South America. Long before, even, there had flourished and waned the two great primordial cultures that bequeathed to the later civilizations the message of their great original style, for the philosophical and aesthetic interpretation of the world: Chavin of Huantar, with its dynamic, poetic, abstract and baroque conceptions, and the great Tiahuanacu with its style of realistic, static, mathematical and concrete expressions. And before them it seems there existed another great civilization, of an equal or superior level to that of the Incas, whose vestiges, dis-

15

covered in the jungles of the Amazon, began to be studied by the Peruvian Julio C. Tello.[18]

Over the imperial ruins of the last Tiahuanacu, during the period of the Cordilleran disorder in which the liberated nations of the Collan empire did battle with each other, the founding of the new Empire of the Sons of the Sun is fulfilled. Its founder was Manco Capac, the Ayar-Manco of the legend, and the founding was achieved by the shadow of the Huanacaure Mount in Cuzco. Departing from their capital, the Sons of the Sun mobilized their expansion towards the four cardinal points, and, finally reached the splendor of the imperial unification. Pachacutec held in those days the reins of the empire, and the rainbow of the Incan flag waved already over practically the whole inhabited area of our continent.

If we summarize everything that has been written about the Incan State and society, we can enumerate its principal characteristics:

— Agrarian collectivism. Paternalistic absolutism. A policy of conquest which utilized peaceful means (persuasion, negotiations), and war only employed as a last resource. Agricultural technology without parallel in the world. Social legislation surpassed only in modern times and only in some aspects. Evolved religion and religious tolerance. A greatly efficient administration based on careful and revised statistics. Excellence of the first order in architecture, ceramics, goldsmithing, education and communications. A highly developed language and a possible writing system whose code has not been discovered, but whose existence is suspected on good authority due to logical proofs and testimonials. Social welfare based on a wise economical and social policy.

Foreign authors—Prescott, and John Collier among others—have subscribed words of admiration for the surprising wisdom of the Incas in exercising complete control over the territory and populations of their vast empire. Both believe that the total and co-operative subjugation could only have been the result of the agreed authority of the governed to express their opinion, and real power wielded by the governing group, to a degree that has no precedent in the history of man.

The political organization of the Empire of the Incas can be compared to a pyramid at whose base was the *puric* or head of the family, and the emperor himself at the apex. Ten puric formed the first grouping, supervised by an official named *Chunca*. A hundred puric formed the auca-puric, governed by the *Pachaca-camayoc*. A *huaranca* consisted of one thousand puric. The grouping of 10,000 puric was known as the *Unu*. Afterwards came the bigger groupings that formed the provinces and the *suyos* or regions in which the empire was divided (Antisuyo, Collasuyo, Chinchasuyo and Cuntisuyo).

16

The cell of the great collectivist empire was the *ayllu*, a family or group of families, who received and enjoyed collectively the land and its products. There was no private property as we know. The land and all means of production belonged to the State. The tillable ground was divided into three parts: for the Sun (for support of the cult), for the Inca (support of the Inca and the government) and for the people. This last part was distributed in strict accordance with the needs of the population, and was revised every year to make the necessary adjustments in harmony with the annual census.

To obtain sufficient production to fulfill the needs of the population, was the big problem which confronted the Incas, after laborious studies to determine the consumption quotas. There were not enough water and land. By means of formidable engineering works to catch the necessary water, and a wise habilitation of the lands (the famous terraces [andenerias]), more solid and longer than the "marvels" of Babylon, it was possible to achieve the difficult objective of equalizing and surpassing the demands of consumption. The undertaking was consolidated with the establishment of graduated compulsory work.

Work was compulsory and idleness was punished as a crime. That apothegm of Paul of Tarsus "who does not work, does not eat", was a rule in that society of producers, in which everyone had access to the welfare paid by his efforts. No one could become rich, but no one could become poor in the empire. When men or nations suffered some misfortune—invalidity, plagues, pestilence—the State gave immediate help. A Spanish conqueror wrote the following eloquent words: "The Incas governed in such a way that they did not have any criminals, thieves or idlers".[19]

The welfare policy of the Incas (everyone must work, no one should overwork, no one should suffer for lack of bread, clothing or shelter), had the assistance of an economy scientifically planned which was based mainly on agriculture. The historians affirm that the agricultural technology of the empire has not been excelled. "Based on the mystical will to live and last, the dense population of the Incan state, with universal accord, made of the conservation and increase of the land resources their national basic policy. Never before then and never since then has any other nation achieved what the Inca state accomplished.[20] The historical success of the Incas, reflected upon the welfare they furnished 20 million people, made anthropologist Roume state: "neither the Greeks nor the Romans, nor the most ancient or most modern civilizations have given us a more perfect example of collectivism".[21]

It is not strange, but logical, that to this economic regime, should have belonged a high juridicial and moral regime. Cieza de Leon and other chroniclers tell of the peaceful laborious life, highly moral, of the indigenous communities they found. That is why the philosopher

Carli could state: "the American Indian was morally superior to the European occidental".[22] There was autocracy, that is true, but a benevolent one, of a paternalistic type, explainable in a society of that epoch. At that time Europe was in its "darkness" of the Middle Ages, and lacked political unity. The Empire of the Incas already enjoyed political-economic unity, and was advancing towards continental unity with Huayna Capac, in an undertaking that was paralyzed by the conquest, but whose ideal persists in the indoamerican conscience.

In the Tahuantinsuyo, besides, there were no human sacrifices, and the war of conquest itself carried with it a civilizing purpose. The vanquished joined the empire with the same responsibilities and rights as the conquerors, keeping their Gods, language and customs in exchange for learning the official language, and accepting a supreme God. For that reason the Incan Empire gave the impression of a vast mosaic of nations and races, sometimes hostile among themselves but following officially the same religion, communicating among themselves in the same official language, joined to the common government, and united, above all, in a conscientious willingness to respect their institutions, and to keep loyalty to the empire and cooperation with the leaders. The empire appears in history as moving like one powerful nation with a solid front, without the vacillations, the retrogression or the failures of the confederations ruled by force or lacking the moral authority delegated by the concensus of the governed peoples.

In ending this short summary of the Incan empire, I quote the accurate words of Haya de la Torre: "The social organization of the Incas is the most extraordinary economic experience of the past. To raise the primitive collectivism, without destroying it, from the tribal type to a great empire, is the same prodigious work accomplished by Nature when it unites the cells, without destroying them, to form tissues and organs".[23]

TEXTUAL NOTES

[1] Teja Zabre, Alfonso, *Historia de México*, E. D. P., México, 1956.

[2] D'Harcourt, Raoul, *América antes de Colón*, E. P., Madrid, 1927.

[3] Von Hagen, V. W., *Realm of Incas*, New American Library, New York, 1927.

[4] Baudin, Luis, *L'Empire Socialiste des Inkas*, Edit. Lux., Paris, 1933.

[5] Thompson, Erick, *México before Cortéz*, Edit. Porrúa, Mexico, 1933.

[6] Keyserling, Conde, *Meditaciones Sudamericanas*, Buenos Aires, 1933.

[7] Magaloni, Humberto, *Reportajes de "Impácto,"* México, Dec., 1958.

[8] Tello, Julio C., *Historia Antigua del Perú*, Ed. San Mart., Lima, 1939.

[9] Posnansky, Arturo, *Tiahuanacu*, E. P. T., New York, 1946.

[10] Morley, Silvanus Griswold, *Historia General de los Antiguos Mayas*, Edit. Porr., Mexico, 1945.

[11] Clavijero, Fr. C., *Storia Antica del Messico*, Casena, 1780.

[12] Collier, John, *Indians of the Americas*, Ed. Mentor, New York, 1958.

[13] Prescott, Will., *Historia de la Conquista del Perú y México*, Modern Library, New York, 1956.

[14] Bennett, Wendell, *Ancient Arts of the Andes*, Museum of Modern Art, New York, 1954.

[15] Keyserling, ob. cit.

[16] Diez de Medina, Fernando, *Letter to Arnold Toynbee*, La Razon, La Paz, Bolivia, July 13, 1951.

[17] Toynbee, Arnold, *Letter to F. Diez de Medina*, La Razon, La Paz, Bolivia, July 13, 1951.

[18] Tello, Julio C., *Objeto y Propósito de la Expedición Arqueológica al Marañón*, Soc. Geográfica, Lima, 1935.

[19] Leguizamon, L., *Testamento*, Cuzco, Perú, 1550.

[20] Collier, John, ob. cit.

[21] Rouma, G., *La Civilization des Incas et leur Communisme Autocratique*, Edit. Ger., Brusels, 1924.

[22] Carli, Don., *Cartas de América*, Rome, 1912.

[23] Haya, Victor R., *Essays*, Lima, 1931.

II

AZTEC

LITERATURE

(Nahuatl language)

PAPER AND WRITING

The existence of books in Pre-Columbian Mexico is no longer a controversial subject. The Aztecs had paper books and knew the science and art of setting their thoughts on paper. Paper and writing, however, were not Aztec inventions, but a legacy from prior civilizations, since all advanced cultures of ancient Mexico used them (the Toltecs, Mixtecas, Zapotecas, Totonecas) and of course the Mayas, who are supposed to have been their inventors more than 2,000 years B.C.

In 1519, Bernal Díaz del Castillo was marching among the Spanish invaders on their way from Veracruz to Tenochtitlan. Progressively as they approached the Anahuac plateau—as he tells us in a fascinating narrative—increasingly definite signs of a powerful aboriginal culture confronted them: impressive architecture, splendid ceramics, and magnificent textile products. And one day, near Cempoala, the invaders were baffled by an unexpected discovery: those "pagan indians" also knew the art of projecting their thoughts by means of the written word. "There is so much to be amazed at, that I don't know how to describe it. . . . When we reached many towns and found the idol shrines and the sacrificers . . . and many paper books folded in the manner of Castillian cloth."[24]

Angel Garibay, glossing the previous words, makes the following comment: "Of course, our exact chronicler Bernal Díaz del Castillo, makes no comment about the contents of those books, but the description he makes of his impressions on first contact with those instruments for the preservation of thought, is indeed very exact. There were books, they were made of paper, and of a paper that the indians had, and used. They were folded like the cloth displayed in the Castillian stores. Thus are the few pre-historic books left to us. The paper, even if it had been used mainly for ritual purposes, was also a means for the transmission of thought. It was fragile, flimsy, delicate, more so in a humid and warm climate like Papantla's and of all Central Mexico. It would not survive like the Egyptian papyri buried under the dry burning sands."[25]

Von Haggen has studied thoroughly the history of paper among the ancient Mexicans. To him belongs the affirmation that the Mayan and Aztec paper was made from the wood of the fig tree, following the simple technique of peeling its bark and beating strips of a certain length with special mallets, until they were pressed into sheets as thin as our present-day paper.[26] "It is like our paper, but theirs is whiter and thicker," wrote Francisco Hernández in 1570, after observing the work of the paper manufacturers of Tetoztlan.[27] It is also known that they had a yellow paper, made from the petiolaris fig tree, and that they used other materials for their manuscripts: cotton cloth, skins, silk, maguey, and aloe leaves.

About the existence of the Aztec books there exists a detailed and conclusive documentation in the correspondence that Fathers Acosta and Tovar had in the XVth Century. (This correspondence was revealed in 1881 by Garcia Icazbalceta)[28] Tovar cleared up three fundamental questions that Acosta had propounded on the subject:

"Q—1. What certainty and authority does this narrative or history possess?

A— Viceroy Enriquez (1568-1580) ordered the compilation of the libraries they had on this matter, and expert historians from Mexico, Texcoco and Tula furnished them to him.

Q—2. How could the indians, without the use of writing (which they did not have) preserve for such a long time the record of so many and varied events?

A— The writing on such books, apparently, must have been figurative, but there are things without a possible direct figuration, therefore "the things that did not have their own image possessed other significative characters, and with these things they represented everything they desired."

Q—3. How can it be believed that the speeches and orations that appear in their history were made by the ancient rhetoricians referred to therein, inasmuch as without letters it does not appear possible that large (and as to their style) elegant speeches, could have been preserved?

A— "In order to keep a complete and verbatim record of the words and plan of the parleys prepared and delivered by the orators, and of the many songs they had—which they all knew by heart even though they expressed them in characters—daily drills were conducted in the colleges attended by the well-to-do youths, in order to preserve them in the same words uttered by the orators and poets. By constant repetition they were retained in their memories without missing a word, selecting the most famous speeches made during a certain period to instruct the youths selected to be rhetoricians. Numerous speeches were retained in this manner, by repetition from person to person until the arrival of the Spaniards, who wrote their speeches and songs in our own writing. Thus they have been preserved."

There existed, therefore, the oral transmission of thought. This was done by experts who applied an original methodology. There existed too the transmission of thought through writing.

Where are, we should ask, the hundreds of Aztec books from the imperial libraries and archives? A few words from Prescott, an authoritative source, give us the answer: "The strange and unknown characters inscribed in the Aztec books stirred tremendous suspicion. They were considered magic parchments and were judged, as were the temples and their idols, as symbols of a pestilent superstition that should be plucked up by the roots."[29] It was for this reason that Juan de Zumárraga, first Archbishop of Mexico, ordered the requisitioning, collecting and burning of all the Aztec books. This example was followed by Spanish leaders and soldiers in every region reached by the invasion. A very few volumes were spared from the flames of this gigantic "auto-da-fe". Some were hidden by the natives, some reached the colonial archives (and used as unserviceable paper according to Sahagun), while a few, the more fortunate ones, were removed from Mexico, and are now in European and North American libraries. Nearly all of them keep the original freshness of their paper, and the brilliant coloring of their illustrations.

Martyr furnished a meticulous description of those Aztec maps that were sent to Spain as soon as the Conquest ended. He felt certain that those maps were conclusive proof of the advanced civilization found in Mexico.[30] Antonio Gama says that: "Bustamante asserted that somewhere in Spain could be found at that time a complete code for deciphering the Aztec system of writing, and that it had been taken to Spain about the time the famous trial against Father Mier was carried out. (1795). According to the author, the name of the Mexican *Champollion* is *Borunda*.[31]

The existing Aztec books have not been completely deciphered. An examination of the Mendoza Codex (perhaps the most important informationally), of the Borgia Collection (with the brightest colored drawings), of the Dresden Codex (the most interesting and perfect according to the experts), and the splendid selection of Sir Kinsborough, leads us to the conclusion, shared by nearly everyone of the historians since Prescott, that those books possess all the elements and characteristics of the most advanced writing system used in the communication of thought.

THE NAHUATL LANGUAGE

Nahuatl was the official language of the empire that reached from sea to sea, from Oxitipan to Xononochco. Clavigero, Sahagun, de la Rosa, Garibay and other authors agree in affirming the excellence of the nahuatl language as a clear, concise, manageable tongue, rich in shades of meaning, harmonious because of the counterpoint of sweetness and gravities of its paroxytone words, and the absence of guttural or nasal sounds. This beautiful and powerful means of expression, capable of resisting the flight of the most abstract thought, had to be, as it was and still is, a splendid instrument for literary creation and its transmission. Nearly all the ancient Mexican literature known to this day, has been transmitted in the Nahuatl language.

On what we can call the map of the Aztec literary production, there appear two outstanding centers in the Central Plateau, the cities of Texcoco and Tenochtitlan. In historical sources, however, we find mention of other centers of literary flowering in Atzcapotzalco, Tlacopan, Cuauhtitlan, the Kingdom of Alcohuacan, Tlaxcala region. It is believed that this literary epoch lasted approximately a century, from the enthronement of Itzcoatl, Fourth Lord of Tenochtitlan, until the Spanish victory of 1521. It is called the Tenoch epoch because it coincided with the apogee and hegemony of Tenochtitlan, and to it belongs all the existing documentation about the aboriginal literature written in the Nahuatl language. But the fact that it is an evolved literature, of ample register, mature realization, and extraordinarily expressive polish, makes one believe that its gestation period springs from ancient cultural origins, and that the sensibility and thought of a complete mosaic of pre-Aztec cultures collaborated in its processing. Until now, among the discernible influences, investigators speak about the contributions of the Huastecos and Otomies, definitely grafted into the literary heritage received, assimilated and self-expressed by the Aztecs.

"Aztec literature reflects in part the feudal type of the style to which its socio-economic organization reached. But we should not generalize. Mayan literature is of sublime lyricism, while the Aztec is of a violent tension. The Mayas live in a mystical anguish with a restlessness of spirit which is beyond knowledge. The Aztecs base their anguish in knowledge itself, in warlike or conquering practices, in their eagerness for unlimited subjugation to their power of all social energies."[32]

The previous words of a well-known Mexican writer reveal in part the truth about the character of the literature bequeathed to us by the successors of the Toltecs and Chichimecs. It is true that this corresponds to the feudal period of Aztec history: literature was used as a dominating instrument and reflects the rigid formalism of the social organization. They became followers of the sublime and dithyrambic style as if they wished to satisfy their thirst for the objectivation of greatness possessed by the feudal group, not only for personal enjoyment, but to impose the people the concept and cult of that greatness.

But there are other elements in Aztec literature; a pathetic anxiety for the liberation of subjugated conscience, a longing to expand life over human limitations, an aggressive tendency to destroy and a contradictory creative restlessness; somber fanaticism and hallucinated mystical impulses; romantic and idealistic bursts facing ungoverned sensualism.

We will find other singular, sometimes contradictory, but always impressive facets of Aztec literature during the study of the literary genre.

SONGS AND DANCES

Poetry, music and dance form the artistic unit best and most cultivated in the heritage the Aztecs bestowed upon us. The song and the dance constituted a type of national institution officered and stimulated by the state, and whose indispensable presence was consecrated by tradition, and was required by the social and political interests in all religious, cultural, agricultural, war and collective activities.

An exceptional witness is Father Durán, who arrived in México shortly after the conquest, and therefore was able to become acquainted with the aboriginal dances and songs in their nearly untouched state, before the interbreeding and the impact of the invasion dimmed their splendor, their authenticity and fine aesthetic quality. He tells us in his story:

"The youths took great pride in knowing how to dance and sing and how to be leaders during the dances. They felt proud of themselves in knowing how to keep time to the music and to execute body movements in unison with the singing. Their dance is not only controlled by the tempo of the music but also by the high and low notes of the chant, singing and dancing together. For these songs, there were among them poets who composed them giving each song and dance different tunes, as we do with our own songs, giving the sonnet, the octosyllabic rhyme and the tercet their different tones for singing . . . etc."

Now follows the interesting report he makes of the various dances:

"There was great variety in their songs and dances, inasmuch as they sang some solemnly and gravely, with great dignity and serenity. These were sung and danced by the gentlemen during formal and official celebrations, singing them with restraint and calm. There were others less serious, known as dances and songs of pleasure, which they called youths' dances. During these they sang songs of love and flirtation as they do to this day when they enjoy themselves. There was still another dance, so picaresque and immodest that it is nearly like that saraband dance our own people perform, with so much wiggling, grimaces and immodest monkeyshines that it could be easily seen that this was a dance of loose women and lewd men. It was called cuecuehcuicatl or "inner itch" dance.[33]

27

Durán continues commenting in his book about many other types of dances and merrymaking, held as much in the temples in honor of the gods as well as in the royal palaces and houses of the nobility, more frequently in the latter, because he adds that the kings and nobles had singers appointed to their courts to compose songs about the greatness of their ancestors and their own. He also makes reference to certain songs and dances called "of relaxation or diversion" which were the basis for the poetical theatricalizations in the temples dedicated to collective recreation:

"The dance they liked best was the one using garlands of roses, with which they crowned and encircled themselves in the main momoxtli of the temple of their god Huitzilopochtli. They used to build a house of roses and constructed artificial trees (or posts) covered with fragrant flowers where they used to seat their goddess Xochiquetzalli. While they danced, young boys disguised as birds and others as butterflies descended from them, adorned with rich green, blue, and yellow plumes. They climbed the trees and skipped from branch to branch sipping the dew from the flowers. Later the gods came forth, each one dressed in his own regalia as they appeared in their altars, and with their blowguns started shooting the fake birds amid the trees. From these trees the goddess Xochiquetzalli used to sally forth to receive them, held them by their hands and sat them next to her, conferring on them much honor and reverence. There they received roses and smoke offerings. Their representatives were also summoned and entertained."[34]

Motolinia, whose commentaries start in 1524, furnishes more detailed comments:

"In the Anahuac tongue the dance has two names: one is *macehualiztli* and the other *netotiliztli*. The latter properly means a dance of rejoicing, with which the indians solaced themselves and enjoyed the pleasure of their own celebrations, in the same manner as the gentlemen and chiefs in their homes and during their wedding feasts. When they dance they say: *netotilo* (they dance), *netotiliztli* (dance). The second and principal name of the dance is known as macehualiztli which properly means "merit". Macehualo means "to merit". This dance was considered as a meritorious deed, as we construe merit in works of charity, of penitence and other virtues directed towards a good purpose. From this verb "macehualo" is derived its compound "tlamecehualo" "for having made penitence or confession." These more solemn dances were held in general feasts and in the private ones. They were also held in the squares or plazas."[35]

The Palatine Manuscript names and classifies the genre. There were songs composed to the style of Huexotzinco, Octoman, Nonoalco, Cazcatlan, Tenican, Cuextlan (modern Aztec), Anahuac (coast), Tepetlan (Chichimecan country), Meztitlan. In other names of these songs we find the ending "cuicatl"—

Teponazcuicatl—with drum accompaniment.

Cihuacuicatl—"women's song" or of men dressed as women.

Atzotzecolcuicatl—girls' song.

Ahuilcuicatl or ixcuecuechcuicatl—"naughly and lascivious songs."

Angel Garibay, in his exemplary work previously cited, has made a study of the Manuscript of Mexican Songs to furnish us with the best classification we have. That classification corresponds to four groups of songs:

1. Poems dedicated to the glorification of heroes and exaltation of war duty:

Cuauhcuicatl—Song of Eagles.

Teuccuicatl—Song of the Princes.

Yaocuicatl—War Song.

The enthusiasm, arrogance, and the impetus of true war mysticism galvanizes the spirit of these poems.

2. Lyric poems of three types—

Xochicuicatl—Song of the Flowers.

Icnocuicatl—Chant of Desolation.

Short Poems.

POETS, MUSICIANS, SINGERS.

Cuicatl is the most common nahuatl equivalent of the word "poem". It is graphically represented by a spiralled word adorned with flowers, which impels one to translate it as the "word in bloom" . . . Garibay points out that it does not mean poem, but "music with words" or without them. This amplifies, but does not invalidate, the first and beautiful poetical significance of the word. Garibay's concept gives us, therefore, a very clear idea of the intimate relationship between music and poetry, and by extension, the possible creative duality of poets or musicians generally called singers, in accordance with the nahuatl word "cuicani" (he who sings or directs the singing) and "cuicapicqui" or "cuicatlazqui" (he who sings, he who composes, he who produces the singing).

Whether only a poet or a musician, a writer of words and melodies, or, according to the huhuatlan denomination, just simply and plainly a "singer", there is no doubt that these creators held high rank in the social scale, formed an institution of traditional privileges, and were stimulated by the state with assistance and honors.

Pomar tells us of the great fondness of the ruling gentlemen for the songs when he says that "the master had time to listen to songs, of which he was very fond because they contained many references to virtue, deeds and exploits of illustrious persons and stories of their past, by means of which they gave encouragement to do great things. They also had other songs of contentment, to pass away the time, and about love."[36] Torquemada[37] refers us to the case of a poet who saved himself from death by composing a poem in his defense and singing it to Netzahualcoyotl. In the great cultural centers of Texcoco and Tenochtitlan they had Singing and Dancing Houses, where those who must have been the singers, dancers and professional actors, used to live, study and rehearse. (Huehuetitlan, Cuicacalitic, Xochicalitic, Xochicalco).

When they celebrated the Feast of the sign L-Flower, they erected two flower poles in front of the palace doors to announce the dancing and rejoicing to the people. "With these they wanted it understood that this was the feast of flowers, to make merry with flowers and to have enjoyment with flowers."[38] On that occasion prizes were awarded and presents and gifts bestowed upon all the general singers, the dance singers, the arrangers of songs, "as well as the holders (those who hold the drum), those who carry and play kettle-drums, those who recite the verses of the song; the composers of the songs, the arrangers and proponents; those who whistle using their cupped hands, those who direct others, those who perform interpretive dances, those who dance in quadrilles, those who intercross breaking the dance, those who sing naughty songs, those who sing funeral dirges, the whirling dancers . . ."[39]

POETRY

The greatest volume of the Aztec literary legacy belongs to poetry, and this is joined to music to form the splendid variety of songs that enrich the manuscripts and codices of aboriginal Mexico. This coupling of verse to melody is a fact as general as the collectivist character of poetry. Individualist poetry never did exist properly, although once in a while, when picking up visions of the surrounding world or expressing the metaphysical anguish for this world and this life's destiny, the poets grafted into the rhythm of choral expression the pathetic notes of their own emotion.

All who have studied Aztec literature—from Durán and Sahagún to Prescott and Garibay—speak of the definite existence of the lyric, epic and dramatic genre. Samuel Brington, in turn, filed certain characteristics which merit revision, but that give a global idea, although incomplete, of the Aztec poetry: "Extreme frequency and richness of metaphors. Greater employment of compound words than in prose. Words and grammatical forms unknown in the vulgar tongue which can be archaic or capriciously constructed by the poet. The vowels are enlarged without regular order whether for emphasis or due to the exigencies of the meter. Interjections are inserted for metric effect and repeated in order to express emotion.[40]

Garibay adds other definite characteristics: Stylistic procedures—parallelism (synonymic, antithetic, synthetic), diphrasism (paired metaphors), refrain.

In so far as the meter, there are these variants:

a) accented and unaccented syllables in three-accent order.

b) accented and unaccented syllables in two-accent order.

c) A series of six syllables with two accents.

d) A verse in two hemistichs, similar to the alexandrine.

e) A combination of hemistichs of Type C with others of Type B.

Garibay mentions a magnificent find: a poetic expression in which to a phrase that varies, corresponds a termination in which the same thought is repeated constantly. Such an expression was used in other aboriginal poems—the Incan among them—and we find it in modern poetry. Here is a typical example:

> Arise, come, be sent; arise, come,
> New-born child,
> Arise, come;
> Arise, come, be sent, arise, come,
> Jewel child,
> Arise, come!

> (Sahagún—Ms. Palat. f. 278 r.)

LYRIC POETRY

As we have already pointed out, it is possible to distinguish three types among the lyric poems:

The Flower Song or *xochicuicatl;* The Chant of Desolation or Sadness, *Icnocuicatl,* and Short Poems of surprising philosophical affinity with the Japanese poetic form of the *tankas* and *haykus.*

The Xochicuicatl is a poem of agile declamation, careful rhythmic unfolding, and predominantly placid tonality. Its expressive beauty has a harmonious union with the philosophical thought of the poet. Sometimes the equilibrium is broken between the outburst of happiness and the philosophical consideration of life and its destiny. The poet then, drowning the joyous expressions for the happiness of the "flowery life," lyrifies his meditations over the transitory nature of life, and flowers, his poetical emblem. The flower is present in the verse, and in all the verse's evolutions, with all the connotations and suggestions of its poetic family of derivatives:

31

The flowers bud, they are fresh, they came into perfect being,
Their petals open . . .
From their bosoms comes forth the florescence of their song!
You, O Singer, scatter them over the world.

(Manuscript of Mexican Songs, F. 33 and f.)

> Let us sing, O Princes,
> Let us please the Life-giver
> With our flower song
> Charmingly blended.
> The flowers were born,
> The Springtime of flowers,
> Under the Sun's rain.
> They are our Heart, O Creator!
> They all long for the possession of your flowers,
> O Creator of Life!
> But they already bear Death's sign
> They are born, they blossom . . . and they die.

(Manuscript of Mexican Songs, F. 14, line 27 and f.)

To the flower and its fascinating repertoire of poetical terms is now joined the melodious suggestion and the plastic splendor that flows from the mention of birds and precious gems. In the following poem, to round up the beauty of the theme, the poet searches for the origin of the flowers and the songs:

> I ask you, O priests
> Whence come the flowers that delight man?
> Whence the enrapturing song, the song that inflames?
> They come only from His Kingdom, Heaven's Soul,
> Only from there they come.
> The singers search for new-born flowers
> As a Sun offering.
> The red corn rains,
> And the birds, clinging to the rushes of Chalco,
> Bring happiness to man.
> Chattering happily over the flowers.
> There is the warbling song thrush,
> The red song thrush of fire,
> And the singing quetzal
> The bright bird of emerald
> Over the emerald pyramids!

(Manuscript of Mexican Songs, F. 34, line 7 and f.)

Of greater splendor and refinement is a poem in honor of Tamoanchan, the mysterious earth referred to by songs, myths and stories, as the Olympus where the Gods created Life, and the legendary womb of poetry.

32

From Tamoanchan, where the flowering tree sinks its roots,
Where the petals softly burst,
From the land of the precious stalk,
Come the dark and the golden birds,
The blue birds and the emerald quetzal.
They come from Nonohualco, land of the thrush,
Next to the sources of waters.
Here come the red macaws of the Sun,
The pink macaws, God's daughters.
The green-blue bird with its florid plume
Is waiting for the dawn, in the region of moss.
The red macaws awakened it
To hear its morning song.

The end of the poem is the most eloquent:

The song is being born, sings the red macaw . . .
And sucks honey.
Let it enjoy delights!
Its heart bursts: it is a flower!

(Manuscript of Mexican Songs, F. 17, line 11 and f.)

Poets and singers arrive at the stoical certainty that life is fleeting, as perishable as everything it creates. They derive two rules for their conduct: to enrapture themselves with life's frenzy until the end, and to impress the memory of their creative power in immortal poems:

We do not come upon this earth a second time,
O Chichimecan Princes!
Let us enjoy life.
That we carry flowers to our death? . . .
Oh well, they are only borrowed.
It is true that we part,
It is quite true, so very true, that we part
We leave the flowers and the songs and the earth
And we are gone forever!

(F. 61, Line 29 and f.)

The *Icnocuicatl*, the Chant of Desolation, is characterized by its elegiac tone, the blows of vehement invocation, and the persistent pathos. It does not possess the serene and wise stoicism of the Xochicuicatl to confront the inexorable realities.—

I cry, I grieve,
It diminishes me to think
That I shall leave the flowers
That I shall leave the song and its rapture.

. . . .

Dost thou suffer, my heart?

33

> It is useless to bear this pain
> We do not live at all upon this earth
> We do not live at all.

(Fragment of F. 35, Line 35 and f.)

The obsession of death, the uncertainty of our final destiny, the future life of those who depart this earth, cover all the themes of the Icnocuicatl, properly named as Songs of Sadness. Here we have another selected fragment:

> Shall I believe this heart?
> Is our destiny, perhaps, upon this earth?
> It is not a place to abide for only a short span,
> A place to live in anguish?
> Perhaps, just like a flower,
> Shall I cast out my seeds
> Or like the corn, begin again within my parents
> And bring forth seed, and thrive upon the world.
> O friends, where is the road to the kingdom of Death,
> The place where one descends, the house of the fleshless?
> Shall we live in the land of mysteries
> Shall our heart be conscious that it lives?

(F. 14, line 23 and f.)

The short poems scattered in the Manuscript of Mexican songs have a different source, but each one of them typifies a lyric genre of surprising characteristics due to its brevity, beauty, suggestion and emotive depths. Here is an example from the Songs of Huexotzinco:

> Will I end as the flowers end?
> Will glory avail me nothing
> My passing through this world,
> Shall it be dust?
> Let me then be flowers
> Or at least be many songs . . .
> What sayest thou, O heart?
> We pass this way, we do,
> All in vain.

(Ms. of Mex. Songs, F. 18, Line 23 and f.)

The following examples, from the manuscript already mentioned, are written in the Nahuatl tongue, but with an unmistakable Otomí keynote, as affirmed by Garibay and supported by other authors after exhaustive investigation.

To the song of a poet—

> Your song is like the blossoming of emeralds
> Or like a nascent flower.

> Mexico's sun can only shine
> Through the flowering of your song.
>
> (Ms. of Mex. Songs, F. 22, Line 22 and f.)

The poet explains his song—

> I cut precious stones,
> I work on gold,
> It is my song.
> I tune my heart,
> I set emeralds,
> It is my song.
>
> (Ms. of Mex. Songs, F. 22, line 26 and f.)

On an ephemeral theme—

> Who says that we live upon the earth?
> It is only a short instant, not forever.
> An emerald will break,
> The glittering gold is into pieces torn,
> The quetzal's brilliant plumage fades away . . .
> We do not live forever
> We are here one fleeting moment, only one.
>
> (Ms. of Mex. Songs, F. 17, Line 15 and f.)

RITUAL POETRY

Under this general title could be grouped all the valuable collection of poems, songs and hymns, of a powerful mystical spirit, emphatic declamation, inciting or admiring, with which the emotion or sentiment of the ancient Mexicans tried to understand their earthly and celestial deities, underscored lyrically the miracle of the "deeds and blessings" of the world, and exalted human actions in the sacred labors of war and agriculture. They are found in the manuscripts of Tlatelolco, Cuauhtitlan, of 1576 or the Aubon Codex, in the Tolteco-Chichimecan History and, in the best examples, in the Manuscript of Tepepulco (Madrid Codex ff.27 to 281). Here we give one dealing with the beloved worship of the corn.

According to a poetic myth, Xochiquetzalli—one of the incarnations of the earthly goddess—dies and descends to the depths of the Hereafter. Her lover, the Child-Prince, or Spring Sun, goes down to search for her and revives her in a son, Cinteotl or Cintli, god of the corn cob. (also Centeutl)

> How bitterly you cried, O priest of the Wind Kingdom!
> The Child-Prince was searching for Xochiquetzalli
> He will come for us to the region of the Turquoise mist.
>
> (Frag. Ms. Palatino 277, p. 54)

35

In the song of Atamalcualixtli that describes the arrival of the earth goddess and of her child-birth, the poet sings under the stars of the sacred night, in front of a multitude:

My heart is a flower: it opens its petals at midnight.
Our mother has arrived,
Our goddess has descended.
Centeutl is born in Tamoanchan
Next to his flowers.
Centeutl was born in the land of the mystery and the rain,
Abode of the flowers,
Where we were created.

(Ms. Palatino F. 279, p. 59)

The god himself sings about his birth:

I am the flowering corn ear with strips of red,
I come into the world.
I am born of the land of the mystery and the rain,
I am a creature of the Sun and of the Earth,
I am their creation,
I have come.

(Ms. of Mex. Songs, F. 27, Lines 16-17)

There is a group of poems already mentioned in the classification of the songs, of lyrical-epic character, whose creation may have been entirely in charge of the "Brotherhood of the Cavaliers of the Eagle" or "The Cavaliers of the Order of the Sun," as Camargo[41] believes: *Cuauhcuicatl*, the Song of the Eagles, *Teuccuicatl*, Song of Princes, and *Yaocuicatl*, or Songs of War.

The following fragments are typical samples of this poetry:

The Fraternity tree
Has its roots on the chest of the Eagles,
Whose blood makes the buds blossom

Sun, Bird of the golden sword,
Resplendent Archer,
Our Creator
Your flight is starting

The first stop will be here
On the vertex of the sacred pyramid,
Then your presence will be scattered
Everywhere,
To shine in the eyes of the Chosen,
To burn in the altars' fire,
To dazzel in the eyes of the Quetzal.

And your golden rain will circulate
In the blood of the Fraternity tree,

36

Whose roots are affirmed
On the Eagles' heart
> (Manuscript of Mexican Songs, F. 17, line 20 and f.)

The sacred fire enliven its red lake,
Its lake of red wings.

O, there you are Chichimecan Princes,
Iztac, Coyotzin and Amecatzin.
Take arrows and shields of the Creator!
Receive the sacred fire!
You love the great flower of fire, don't you?

Let's go ahead!
Quietly offer the gladness of your death
Calmly glorify the flying Eagle!

Here are the drums,
Ready are the flowers,
Brought by Tateocinteulitli,
the Chichimecan.
> (Manuscript of Mexican Songs, F. 32, line 1 and f.)

There is nothing like to die at fight.
There is nothing like the bloomed death,
The bloomed death on the battle field!

It is beautiful for the one who dies.
It is beautiful for the chosen hero.

I forsee death very far yet,
But near or far, I say, it is inmaterial
For my heart, which never trembles.

My heart will tremble one day, however
It will be feeling the great emotion,
The sacred emotion of the Chosen,
The glorious chosen man to die,
To die and bloom at the battle field!
> (Manuscript of Mexican Songs, Ex. F. 66, line 1 and f.)

EPICS AND HISTORY

With the recent investigations and interpretations of the cultural life of the aboriginal civilizations, it is easier the comprehension of the eloquent words spoken by Alfonso Caso in 1949: "The natives, not only in Mexico, but in all Meso-America, possessed a real historical vocation, and narrated and wrote history."[42]

The existence of the vocation presupposes the development of a science and the perfecting of a methodology plus a concept of history

Our aborigines had a concept of history not lacking in modernity to the concept of Bernheim: "a science that studies and expounds, in causal connection, the facts of the development of man in his manifestations as a social entity." For them history was the genetic narration of man's development and of his social group across time and space. This fact, so clear in the Popol-Vuh of the Maya-Quichés, can only be half-proven in the epic poetry and the narratives in prose of Aztec literature, due to the dispersion or mutilation of the manuscripts, to the confusion of the study materials, and to the lack of an organic book, of uninterrupted sequence, like that admirable National History of the Quichés. Nevertheless, there is an essential fact on which the scientific conclusions rush to confirm the brilliant and bold asseverations of Rafael Girard about the essentially mythological character of our aboriginal cultures, and around the perpetuation of the cultural mythical arquetypes, until the present day, of native life: "The indian still lives in a mythical age, the fourth of his cyclography, that is, in a sacred space and time, which reveals that his culture has remained impervious to occidental influence, and that the explanation of the cultural phenomena lies in the myths."[43]

For the Maya-Quichés, and by extension for the Aztecs and Quechuas, there is a sort of mythical code, secular in several instances, from which start the conceptions, the rites, life's practices, the conduct and destiny of our contemporary indians. In order to know the indian of today, and delve deeply into his cultural complexes, there is no truer way than the study and interpretation of his myths. The task is possible if we remember that "the myths find a clear explanation in the conceptions and practices of the indian of today. All their acts, individual and collective, including the physiological ones, are rites that repeat continuously the mythical models."

Our indians, then, had a historical vocation and forged the body of ruling myths for the evolution of a culture whose fluent, dynamic, selective and actualizing history, in a task requiring a millennium, is demonstrating the truth, some times slanted, that a culture—all culture—is not, and cannot be, but the whole of its history. It was thus understood by the Aztecs.

The history of the Mexican aborigines, that we might well call the great mytho-history of the native Mexico, was forged and transmitted word by word and by writing. For the oral transmission there existed special institutions like the Calmecac, about which so much is told to us by Sahagún in his history, with a program of studies which gave special importance to the teaching of history through songs and oratory. The apprenticeship started at 10 years of age, and used the nemotechnic method preponderantly. The Teucuicatl, or the Song of the Gods held first place, next came the songs to the numens, to the founders, and to the warrior leaders. Other chapters of the culture were inserted: the Tonalpoalli, the indian astrology and the magic calendar, the Temicamatl or interpretation of dreams, the Xiuhamatl which contained the annals of the empire or book of the years.

Memory, well trained and better used, was the great aid that the aboriginal educators utilized to ensure the survival of their historical magnificence, from generation to generation. With a great pedagogical sense they used music to make the work more 'agreeable or galvanize remembrance; they used graphic representations to guide the apprenticeship and recitation phases; of painting to maintain interest, stimulate comprehension and fix the succession of facts and dates. That this method was very effective is evidenced by the formidable oral transmission collected by Tezozomoc in his Mexicoyotl Chronicle. The sage Max Muller assures us that this nemotechnic method, wisely applied, has achieved surprising results, when he demonstrates that the Veda texts have been transmitted orally for more than two thousand years, and so accurately, that a doubtful accent barely exists in its whole extension.[44]

Due to adverse circumstances, the whole wealth of epic has not reached us in the nahuatl tongue. But we can depend on the Manuscript of 1528, the one from Cuauhtitlan, the Tolteco-Chichimecan History, the 1576 Manuscript, the Aubion Codex, the Mexicoyotl Chronicle, Volume II of Sahagún's History, the Narratives of Ixtlilxóhitl and, especially, the famous Legend of the Suns which contains such suggestive chapters as these: The New Creation of Man, the Poem of the Suns, the Creation of Corn, The Mimixcos, The Creation of the Sun, the Conquests of Quetzalcoatl.

Like the style of the epic of other aboriginal cultures, the Aztec epic has a record that starts from the creation of the world until the final flowering of the civilizations. The epic commentary places emphasis on the exploits of the first generation of creators, founders and civilizers, among them Quetzalcoatl—the one with the most impressive biography and most extensive poetic fabulousness— and underscores the pregrinations and vicissitudes of the nations that meet. flowing from the four cardinal points, to forge the great constellation of cultures that flourished in the sacred plateau of Anahuac.

We quote below the poem that sings of the arrival of Quetzalcoatl at the sea shore, ending his legendary flight, to live the grand moment of the glorious transformation:

> *When he arrived at the shores of the divine sea,*
> *To the edge of the luminous ocean, he paused and wept.*
> *Took his jewels and vestments and donned them,*
> *His crest of quetzal plumes, his mask of turquoises,*
> *And when he was all adorned, he set himself afire,*
> *And burst into flames!*
> *It is for this reason that the place where Quetzalcoatl burned,*
> *Is called the Quemadero, the burning place.*

It is said that when he was ablaze,
When his ashes were beginning to rise,
All the precious birds came down to see him,
The brilliant-plumed birds that know the heavens,
The red macaw, the bee eater, the thrush,
The resplendent white bird, the green-pink parrots
And macaws with the hues of the rainbow.
When his ashes no longer burned,
Quetzalcoatl's heart began its flight.
They saw him fly to heaven, settle there,
And change into a star.
Since then he is called Quetzalcoatl,
He who reigns at dawn

(Ms. of Cuauhtitlan pp. 3-4)

DRAMATIC POETRY
AND THE THEATER

In talking about dances and songs we quote Durán on a lovely type of dance "the one best liked by the Mexicans", which was held at the main momotzli of the temple, presided by Xochiquetzalli "goddess of the roses". The words above quoted refer to the introit of a performance in which "they brought an indian dressed like the goddess." This indian was made to sit at the temple steps and a woman's loom was placed on his hands. He was forced to weave in the same manner as the women weave, and he made believe he was weaving. While thus occupied all the other officials danced (disguised as monkeys, cats, dogs, coyotes, lions, tigers), a very pleasant dance, each bearing in his hands their insignia of office: the silversmith carrying his instruments, the painter his brushes and colored bowls. . . .

The same author furnishes us with information on the following dance: "There was another dance of old men who donned masks of hunchbacked old men. This dance is quite elegant and lively and very funny. Similarly, there was a dance and song of jugglers or buffoons during which they introduced a simpleton who faked misunderstanding his master's orders and inverted his words." "At other times they performed certain dances where they painted themselves black or white or green, adorning their heads and feet with feathers, carrying off some women in the meanwhile, all of them pretending drunkenness, carrying small pitchers and cups in their hands as if for drinking. All this was feigned to give pleasure and comfort to the cities, enlivening them with many types of games invented by some of the assemblage (most probably by the priests and teachers of the Calmecac). These included joyful dances, farces, interludes and ballads.[45]

Durán reveals at this time the existence of certain authors belonging to what we could possibly call the primitive farce or "pleasure theater", a term he likes to repeat so much. They were the inventors of the one-act farce, small plays, primitive ballets, theatrical genre of either burlesque or allegoric type. These were prepared for either public or private diversion. But he also tells us about another group of singers or troubadours at the service of the great lords, engaged to sing of exploits and greatness, and also of a third group of authors who lived in the temples, earned fees and were the creators of songs for the gods. The name given to them was *cuiccapique* or "composers of songs." Remembering that poetry was generally joined to music, and that the song preceded the dance, a solidary artistic reality in all aboriginal societies, the compositions of the private singers and of the imperial cuiccapiques are definite antecedents—if not the first samples —of the profane and religious theater, as are, without doubt, the poetical competitions of the nobles; and are already grand theatrical creations of magnificent technique, complicated ritual and dramatic action, those that correspond to the feasts of Tlacaxipehualixtli, Texcatl, Teci, Xochiquetzalli and others told in detail by Sahagún.[46]

The study of the theatrical characteristics of the epic and collective ballads, the ballets of allegoric type and public showing, the dramatization of the gallant history of heroes and gods, the monologues, dialogues and colloquies of a lyrical or epic theme, the collective and haughty narration of the great historical events of the community; all merit a special undertaking. Angel Garibay, in his monumental work, proclaims the authenticity of the dramatic literature in the Nahuatl tongue, especially the one studied in the Manuscript of Mexican Songs, and assures, on good authority, that there is no antecedent in Spanish literature of the original technique developed by the aboriginal dramatists. This technique consists of presenting the theme in a series of dramatic sketches "a succession of melodramatic sequences", comparable only to certain moving picture continuities, where only the essence of thoughts and emotions are portrayed in the least number of words, and with the greatest economy of action. That is to say, they were doubly representative, for their agile technique and for depicting the emotion of the deed itself.[47]

Garibay presents us an example in wide and bold strokes, not the most characteristic, but possibly one having the greatest literary beauty. It is entitled *Icuic* Netzahualcoyotl, in four stages:

1. Prelude of a singer: Invitation to sing and an evocation of Netzahualcoyotl.
   Netzahualcoyotl speaks—

   > I, Netzahualcoyotl, weep
   > With what shall I go?
   > With what shall I perish?

41

(The song continues about the same theme)

Another poet replies—

> *Only the song can be our shroud,*
> *The warriors destroy our books.*
> *To think there is joy here!*
> *No one has a home in this world,*
> *We must leave the enchanting flowers.*

(The invocation to the king continues)

2. *The king sings alone.* (Beautiful metaphors: my heart feels like a perfumed flower—the flower of the song breaks within my heart).

3. Dialogue between two disguised singers (a macaw and a quetzal)

> *Macaw:* *I, a red-yellow macaw, flew*
> *I flew over the earth,*
> *My heart was enraptured.*

> *Quetzal:* *I am the quetzal*
> *I sing among the flowers*
> *I sing under the divine rain,*
> *I give my song, my heart is in ecstasy.*

> *Macaw:* *The water blossoms,*
> *Its foam blossoms over the earth,*
> *My heart is full of rapture.*

> *Quetzal:* *I am saddened, afflicted, I weep*
> *The earth is a home for no one.*
> *I am a Mexican and I say, Forward!*
> *Let us go to Tehuantepec,*
> *The Chiltepec perishes,*
> *Tehuantepec weeps.*

> *Macaw:* *O Mexican, my friend, do not be annoyed,*
> *Let him of Chiltepec perish,*
> *The star of Death shall fall on him,*
> *Let him of Xochitlan perish*
> *Let him of Amaxtlan weep,*
> *As the one from Tehuantepec weeps.*

4. Three voices and an epilogue (One voice is that of a poet. The theme is: Ephemeral life. The second voice belongs to Netzahualpilli. The third one is that of a captive praising the king. The epilogue is sung by all.) From this part is extracted the following excerpt:

> *There where dawn is, the light weaves your dwelling.*
> *Your flowers open their petals like emeralds*
> *Your song is like a slow rain of jewels.*

42

PROSE LITERATURE

There still remained the great bulk of knowledge, experiences, political, religious, civic and moral events whose recording and transmission did not fit the songs, the lyric and epic poetry, or the theater. Prose took charge of this group, a meticulously elaborate prose in order to be able to give expression to the valuable material poured into it. This literature in prose, composed, organized and transmitted under norms of great pedagogical sense, had eminently educational ends, and utilized two styles to adapt itself better to the temper of the themes dealt with. One was a plain style, choppy, laconic, to register time, space and sequence of events and actions. The other, a purely literary one, was adapted for sober, persuasive narrations dedicated to youth, for use in harangues and parleys, in the dialogues of old men, in the sparkling plot of the fables, riddles, short stories and adventures of the gods. It is in the latter style that we find a prose abounding in parallelisms, synonymies, diphrasims, and the classic narrative technique of the type followed in motion pictures.

Surely one of the most estimable legacies is the one of *Huehuet-lacelli* or Talks of the Old Men (which are believed to have been collected by P. Olmos), of which a complete manuscript exists in the Library of Congress in Washington, and another in the National Library of Mexico (with only the first two talks). Among the printed are the following—of Juan Bautista, 1600, Brown Library, Peñafiel 1901. The "Talks" form a charming succession of persuasive discourses to guide, channel or correct human and social conduct. The following titles can give an idea of the great repertoire of themes:

—Talk of a mother to her daughter giving her advice.

—Admonition given by a father to his young son.

—A reply from a wife to her husband.

—Talk to the chiefs of Tlaxcala about the government of their city, so they will not fail, and be able to govern their republic well.

—Talk to those walking to school.

—Advice from a father to his son after his marriage.

Please note in the following excerpts the polished and plain expression, always convincing, the eloquence of the reasonings, and the selected precepts for domestic and social education:

Caution in talking

—In this be very careful, watch yourself well about the use of lascivious and garrulous words. They are not good or proper. They provoke people to lust. They can, without one knowing, damage, smear and provoke lasciviousness.

From a father to his son, about women.

—And be careful about undue desiring and coveting "the chemise" and "the skirts". It perverts, debases and taints people. You are yet pristine water, you are only a fledging, still budding, a young spike of growing grass. You are like fine jade, like a turquoise, or like the fine plume of a quetzal. Do not, through your own actions and desires, bleed and flay yourself. Somewhere chemises and petticoats are always lying in waiting. Yours is youth now. Grow, bring forth buds over the earth. Do not hurry.

(Olmos, Manuscript No. 27)

Behavior while listening to an admonition.

—And when someone may be admonishing you, do not amuse yourself with other things, don't hold any plaything in your hands. Do not play with your feet as if you were not paying attention. Do not nibble the edges of your robe. Do not spit. Do not move your head from side to side. Do not stand up suddenly. I advise you not to do these things. Do them and you shall be known as a knave.

(Olmos—Ms. No. 27)

From a mother to her daughter.

—Do not make friends with liars, thieves, dissolute women, frequenters of houses, or lazy women, so you will not be affected or corrupted by them. Do not show yourself at the door, or loiter in the market place, on the road, or near the water. They are not good places. There lurks shame, perversion, what brings difficulties and misery to people; what degenerates them. There lurks evil and perversion.

—Govern well your sown land, your seeded fields, and take good care of your laborers. Safeguard well your trunk, your box, and close well your pot and your bowl.

—Don't spend dissolutely, do not destroy or ruin yourself. If you are going away continuously, if you are always coming and going, you will never see your pots or bowls again, nor by living this way will you own quarters, or your own home.

How to treat a husband.

—If he lives with you, you shall cuddle him on your lap and hold him in your arms. Do not try to lord it over him like an eagle or like a tiger . . . In peace and quietness you shall tell him about the things he does to you that cause you pain. Do not tell him in front of others or you shall shame him.

About adornments.

—Do not oversearch for, nor always desire or want beautiful adornments. Do not comb your hair continuously or look at yourself in the mirror all the time. Do not fix yourself or primp continuously. Do not always desire beautiful finery.

(Olmos—Ms. F. 132)

The sixth volume of Sahagún's Natural History is a veritable mine of admirable examples, divided into four groups according to their subject: invocations and talks with the gods; pieces of regal and political oratory; counselling and teaching by the kings to their heirs; parley and traditional ceremonies for the selection of a wife; about pregnancy, childbirth, etc., etc. Sahagun entitles this part of his book: "the rhetoric, moral philosophy and theology of the Mexican people . . . where we find many curious things about the elegance of their language and many delicate things about the moral virtues."[48] From this monumental book we have extracted the following samples:

Informal lecture to Tlatoacni.

"See that you receive with affability and humbleness those who may appear before you in sadness and in trouble. You should not do or say anything rashly. Listen with calmness and completely the complaints and information they give. Do not cut short the words and reasons of the speaker. Be careful that you don't accept persons lightly, or punish someone without reason, because the power to punish is God-given. It should be used like the nails and the teeth of God to dispense justice. You are his executor, prosecutor and judge."

(Book VI, Chap. X, 439)

Sexual education.

"Do not throw yourself over a woman like a dog over his food. Do not be like a dog when eating and swallowing what is thrown to him. Do not give yourself to women prematurely. Even though you desire a woman, control your heart until you have become a man."

"Look at the maguey plant: if they open it when it is young to take away its honey, neither does it have or will give honey, but shall die. Before they open it to obtain its honey they let it grow and let it reach its perfection. Only then is its honey gathered, in season and in due time."

(Ob. cit. Chap. XXI, I, 551)

––––––––––

Angel Garibay printed in Tlalocan, in 1943, a work that brought to life a document of the XVII—Century, and which now forms part of the Bancroft Library of the University of California. Because of its miscellaneous title he named it *Huehuetlatolli.*

The untiring Sahagún brings us curious news about the taste, skill and mastery with which the ancient Mexicans invented riddles, coined proverbs, and polished metaphors of fine and deep suggestion. In the titles he dedicates to them (Book VI, Chap. XLI to XLIII) he writes about some adages "that these Mexican people used", of the "Zazaniles" or riddles, and about "some delicate metaphors". Here are some riddles:

"Guess this: Ten stones that somebody has to carry. (They are finger nails)."

"Guess this: A white stone from which green feathers grow. (It is the onion plant)."

"Guess this: A jumping red-ochre stone. (It is the flea)."

There is ample testimony that a very important part of the prose was dedicated to the chronicles and historical narratives. They are not of the same type and style, naturally. The chronological register of the historical events, transcribed from the pictograph on which it was fixed by the Anahuac sages, is moderate, direct and plain:

"Year 6—House—At this time the Mexicans completed four years in Pantitlan. Diseases spread among them. All their bodies were chapped.

"10   Flint—Chimalpopoca died. The Tecpanecas carried him away.

"13   House—It was icy. The growing corn shoots were burned. The beginning of man."

In the following sample from the Cuauhtitlan manuscript we find the same moderate style. It has, however, gained in its descriptive quality.

Year 10—House—At this time Huactli, King of Cuauhtitlan, died. This was the king who did not know how to plant edible corn. His subjects did not know how to weave robes. They wore no other clothing than skins. Their food still consisted of birds, snakes and rabbits. They did not live in houses and travelled aimlessly, wandering.

Year 10—Flint— The Chichimecas tied Queen "Leather Petticoats". They shot her with arrows in a place known as Calacohuayan. The reason the Chichimecas were angered was because the Colhuacans had made her a harlot."

History was followed step by step in this typical register of particular events and was enlarged, explained and its literature beautified in the narratives and the songs, the greater part of which still awaits classification and interpretation in the priceless documents of the Tolteco- Chichimecan History, the Mexicayotl Chronicles, the Tecamachalco Annals, the Manuscripts of 1576, of Cuauhtitlan and of Tlatelolco (Part III).

In his prologue to the History of the Chichimecan Nation, the words of Ixtlilxochitl give some idea of the materials used by the Nahuatl historians, about the organization and division of the literary and scientific work, and about the methodological classification of the materials of the extensive works of the poets, writers and sages of Anahuac.

—"The histories were developed with pictures and characters with which they were written and memorized, as they were painted at the time when the events happened."

—"Songs by means of which serious authors in their mode of learning and skill, preserved them.

—They had writers for each genre: some dealt with annals, arranging in order the things that happened every year, noting down the day, month and hour.

—Others were in charge of genealogies and descent of kings, lords and persons of lineage, entering by count and name those who were born, and deleting those who died by the same procedure.

—Some had charge of the pictures of the metes, bounds and landmarks of the cities, provinces, towns and places, and the distribution of lands, entering the names of the tenants or owners.

—Others kept the legal ritual and ceremonial books.

—And, finally, the philosophers and sages, among them, were charged with the task of depicting all the sciences they knew and achieved, and with the teaching of all songs they preserved."

––––––––––

It is not necessary to insist about the creative potentialities of the ancient Mexicans after this brief review of their literature. These potentialities shone in the splendid creative work of the theological and cosmogonical myths, whose dynamic and directing constellation appears guiding the human and social happenings, from the first to the last aboriginal horizon. (Please read for greater certainty the Legend of the Suns [Manuscript of 1558], The Creation of the Maguey [Olmos, Manuscript of 1543] and those of the History of the Mexicans through their Pictures [O. Book of Mendieta] with the creation of music, man, fire, and earth).

For minds endowed with this creative capacity, it was not extraordinary, but natural, to delve in other forms of purely imaginative narrative, or of an alliance between fantasy and reality. They cultivated the legend, the fable, the tale, the anecdote and a type of novel whose reconstruction unfortunately has not been accomplished yet. As examples we have the Istac Tototl or White Bird (Cuauhtitlan Manuscript), The Girl of the Alders (from the same manuscript) and the Adventures of Netzahualcoyotl.

When, if possible, all this rich archive of literature written in the nahuatl tongue is assembled—it is at present scattered in libraries all over the world—and a group of scholars be willing to assume the formidable task of arranging, classifying and interpreting its texts, we will be able to obtain a wider and definite view of what the man of the different cultures was able to create and perpetuate. From what has been stated and expounded, there exists sufficient ground to re-assure us in our conviction that the Aztec literature, by its aesthetic quality and its creative orbit, is not below the quality of any litera-ture either ancient or contemporaneous.

For those authors who, without any justification, eliminate the chapter of aboriginal literatures in the history of American Literature, and for those literary critics whose occidental optics do not want or cannot encompass our Pre-Columbian cultural horizon, the following well-aimed words of the Mexican Andrés Henestroza have been written:

"The critics make themselves this reflection: How can culture exist where it ignores the true God? How can you call painting, sculp-ture, architecture, and literature things dedicated to a "barbaric" cult? From this basis they deny all indigenous manifestations, because there is not a single cultural indigenous manifestation that does not have a religious content. And inasmuch as the Conquest persecuted all those manifestations, precisely because of their religious content, the medie-val and colonially-minded writers, who have not been able to over-come religious prejudice, persist in thinking that there is no indigenous literature, that the literature was born when Tenochtitlan fell. Some writers like José Vasconcelos have averred that the Spaniards did not "destroy" anything, because there was nothing worthy of preservation. It is precisely Sahagún who, foreseeing all that mob of deniers, stated beforehand that whoever thought that what he had said was his own invention, he could only answer that: *human understanding cannot invent the spirit of a people.*"[49]

48

TEXTUAL NOTES

[24] *Bernal Diaz del Castillo,* Historia Verdadera de la Conquista de México, Edit. Mex, Mexico, 1949.

[25] A. M. Garibay, *Historia de la Literatura Nahuatl,* Edit. Porrúa, México, 1953.

[26] V. Van Haggen, The Aztec: man and tribe, New American Library, New York, 1959.

[27] Francisco Hernández, *Rerum Medicarum Novac Hispaniae The saurus seu Pantarum,* Rome, 1649.

[28] Garcia Icazbalceta, documentación a la *Biografía de Zumárraga.* Vol. IV, pag. 89-95. Edit. Porrúa, Mexico, 1947.

[29] W. Prescott, *The Conquest of México,* Harpers and Brothers, New York, 1843.

[30] Peter Martyr, *De Orbe Novo,* Compluti, 1530.

[31] Gama, Descripción. México, 1890.

[32] Arqueles Vela, *Evolución Histórica de la Literatura Universal,* México, 1942.

[33] P. Durán, *Historia de las Indias de Nueva España,* Mexico 1867-80. Pag. 230.

[34] id. id. pag. 231.

[35] Motolinia, *Memoriales,* pag. 344, Paris, 1903.

[36] Pomar, *Documentos para la Historia de México* (reproducido by Garcia Icazbalceta), México, 1947.

[37] Torquemada, *Monarquía Indiana* (I-165-b), Madrid, 1723.

[38] *Manuscrito Palatino,* F.202, pag. 303.

[39] id. id.

[40] Samuel Brinton, *Ancient Nahuatl Poetry,* Filadelfia, 1987.

[41] Camargo, *Historia de Tlaxcala,* México, 1930.

[42] *El Mapa de Teczacualco,* pag. 145, México, 1949.

[43] Rafael Girard, *El Popol Vuh,* fuente historica, Vol. I, Edit. Min. Educación Pública, Guatemala, 1952.

[44] Max Muller, *La Ciencia de la Religión,* Edit. Albatros, México, 1945.

[45] P. Durán, ob. cit., II, pp. 196 y 233.

[46] Sahagún, *Historia General,* II, pp. 281 y 189, México.

[47] Garibay, ob. cit., pp. 196 y 355.

[48] Sahagún, ob. cit. Libro VI.

[49] Henestroza, Revista *Universidad de México,* México, Abril, 1952.

—*Amoxcalli*. Libraries of the ancient Mexico.

—*Atamalcualiztli*. Holiday devoted to the God of the Rain. The people used to eat "tamales" without condiment on this day.

—*Calmecac*. Academies of Arts and Sciences for priests and nobles.

—*Centeotl*. God of the "Green Corn."

—*Cuauhcihuatl*. Woman-Eagle. Another name of the Goddess-Mother.

—*Cuauhzochamati*. Documents of the land boundaries.

—*Cuicatl*. General word for "song with musical accompaniment". With its stem many other words are formed: *cuicanqui*, inventor of songs; *cuicaito*, he who sings and recites them; *cuicani*, the singer in general; *cuicapicque*, the one who dances; *cuicacalli*, the house of songs.

—*Cuauhcuicatl*. The song of the Eagles.

—*Cihuacuicatl*. Women's songs.

—*Huehuetl*. Small drum.

—*Huehuetlatolli*. Talks of the old men. Lessons on moral, civic, social, and religious education.

—*Icnocuicatl*. Chant of Desolation.

—*Itzpapaloti*. Night-Goddess. Another name of the Goddess-Mother.

—*Macelhualcuicani*. "Singer that sings and dances".

—*Macelhualiztli*. Dance to "ingratiate one's self with the Gods".

—*Mictlan*. Region for those died by common death.

—*Mixcoacalli*. Place for marital songs and war dances.

—*Nanotzin*. Literally means "motherhood". Main name of the Goddess-Mother.

—*Oceloti*. Puma or tiger. In the symbology the *oceloti* represents the Earth, while the eagle represents the sun.

—*Octli*. Juice of the "maguey". Now is named "pulque".

—*Otoncuicatl*. Song of Otomi style.

—*Papalocalitec*. Literally "House of the butterflies". It was used to name one of the meeting places of the poets.

—*Pilcuicatl*. Children's songs.

—*Quetzacoatl*. Name used for a God as well as for an historic personage and a high eclesiastic dignity in Tenochtitlan. Literally means "feathered serpent" (with quetzal feathers).

—*Quetzal*. Sacred bird.

—*Tamoanchan*. Sacred region where the dead people live, the "descarnados" or "those removed from earthly things" and that some day will return to the world. Other meaning is: the olympus where Gods created life and the legendary womb of poetry.

—*Tecuhamati*. Book for the chronology and events of the kings.

—*Telpochmacehualiztli*. Dance of the young unmarried men.

—*Teponazcuicatl*. Song with drum accompaniment.

—*Telpuchcalli*. Public schools.

—*Tepehualamoxtli*. History of conquests.

—*Teyocoyani*. Creator of men.

—*Tlacalaquilamati*. Taxes record book.

—*Tlacamecayoamati*. Book of the kings' genealogy.

—*Tlacatlaolli.* The sacred food for the people chosen as victims of the religious sacrifices.

—*Tlacuilo.* Scribe devoted to write the annals.

—*Tlaloc.* Divinity of the Earth. There was a "tlaloc" for each of the cardinal points

—*Tlalocan.* Paradise of the God of the Life and the Rain.

—*Tlapalli.* Colored ink to paint the symbols expressing thoughts.

—*Tlilli.* Black ink. Also means *writing*.

—*Xaocuicatl.* War song.

—*Ximoayan.* Synonym of Tamoanchan.

—*Xochicalli.* Another name for the meeting places of poets.

—*Xochicuicatl.* Song of the flowers.

—*Xochiquetzalli.* Goddess of the pleasures.

—*Yohuallahuana.* God of the masculine fertility.

—*Yoloticlue.* Goddess of love.

GENERAL BIBLIOGRAPHY

Acosta, José de, *Historia Natural y Moral de las Indias*, Sevilla, 1959.

Alva Ixtlilxochitl, Fernando de, *Obras Historicas: 1. Relaciones*, México, 1891; 2. *Historia Chichimeca*, Mexico, 1892.

Aubin, J. M., *A Memoires sur la peinture didactique et L'escriture figurative des ancients Mexicaines*, Paris, 1885.

Baptista, Juan, *Huehuetlatolli o Pláticas de Viejos*, México, 1599.

Barlow, Robert H., *El códice de los alfareros de Cuauhtitlan*, Revista Mexicana de Estudios Anropologicos, XII, Mexico, 1955.

Boturini, B., *Idea de una Historia General de la América Septentrional*, Madrid, 1746.

Brington, D. G., *Ancient Nahuatl Poetry*, Philadelphia, 1871.

Campos, Ruben, *La producción literaria de los Aztecas*, México, 1936.

Caso, Alfonso, *La Religion de los Aztecas*, Mexico, 1937.

————, *El Arte Prehispanico*, México, 1940.

Castillo Ledon, Luis, *Antigua Literatura Indigena Mexicana*, México, 1917.

Clavigero, F. J., Historia Antigua de México, México, 1945.

Diaz del Costillo, Bernal, *The New History of the Conquest of New Spain*, Hakluyt Society, 5 vol., London, 1908-16.

Durán, Diego, *Historia de las Indias de la Nueva España*, 2 vol., and atlas, 1867-1880, Mexico.

Garcia Icazbalceta, J., *Nueva Colección de Documentos para la Historia de México*, 5 vol., 1886-1892.

Garibay, A. M., *Historia de la Literatura Nahuatl*, 2 vol., Edit. Porrúa, Mexico, 1953.

Kroeber, Alfred L., *Archaic Culture Horizons in the Valley of Mexico*, University of California, Publications in American Archeology and Etnology, Vol., 17, Berkeley, 1927.

Leal, Luis, *El Códice Ramirez*, Revista Mexicana, III Mexico, 1953.

Lenz, Hans, *El Papel Indigena*, Mexico, 1950.

Ludexis, H. E., *The American Aboriginal Languages*, London, 1858.

Miranda, E., *Algunos Comentarios Botánicos* (acerca de la fabricación del papel por los Aztecas), Cuadernos Americanos, México, 1946.

Monzon, Arturo, *El Calpulli en la Organización de los Tenochca*, Mexico, 1940.

Motolinia, F. Toribio, *Historia de los Indios de Nueva España*, Barcelona, 1914.

————, *Memoriales*, Paris, 1903.

Olmos, F. Andres, *Arte para Aprender la Lengua Mexicana*, Paris, 1875.

Paso y Troncoso, Francisco de, *Leyenda de los Soles*, Biblioteca *Nahuatl*, Florencia, 1903.

Peñafiel, Antonio, *Cantares Mexicanos*, cop. phot., Manuscript of the Mexican National Library, México, 1904-1906.

————, Colección de Documentos para la Historia Mexicana, México, 1897-1903.

Prescott, William, *The Conquest of México*, American Library, New York, 1952.

Reko, B. P., *El Arbol del Papel en el México Antiguo*, Botanic Society of America, Vol. 5, México, 1947.

Rosny, L., *Les Documents Ecrits de l'Antiquite Americaine*, Paris, 1882.

Sahagún, Bernardino de, *Historia General de las Cosas de la Nueva España,* Ed. Acosta Saignes, 3 vol., Mexico, 1946.

————, *El Libro de los Coloquios de los Doce con los Satrapas,* Mexican Review of Historical Studies, Mexico, 1924.

Simeon, Remi, *Dictionaire de la Langue Nahuatl,* Paris, 1885.

Spence, L., *The Mythologies of Ancient México and Perú,* London, 1907.

Tezozómoc, Fernando, *Crónica Mexicana,* Ed. Vigil, México, 1878.

Torquemada, Juan, *Los Veintiun Libros Rituales y Monarquia,* 3 vol., Madrid, 1723.

Toscano, Salvador, *Fuentes para la Historia de México:* 1. *Historia Tolteco-Chichimeca,* Mexico, 1947; 2. *Anales de Ttatelolco,* México, 1948.

————, *Arte Precolombino,* México, 1944.

Tovar, Juan, *Historia de los Indios Mexicanos,* Edit. Vigil, Mexico, 1878.

Tozzer, Alfred N., *The Value of Ancient Mexican Manuscripts,* in the study of the general development of writing, Edit. Smithsonian Institute, Washington, 1912.

Valentini, D. J., *Fabricación y Usos del Papel entre los Antiguos Mexicanos,* Worcester, 1880.

Zapata y Mendoza, J. V., *Historia Cronológica de la Nación Tlaxxalteca,* Col. Goupil, Ms. No. 212, National Library, Paris.

Zurita, Alonso de, *Breve y Sumaria Relación de los Señores de la Nueva Espana.,* Garcia Icazbalceta, Colección de Documentos para la Historia, 2nd. Edit., México, 1942.

CODICES—Manuscripts

Anales de Tecamachalco, Edit., Peñafiel: "Documentos para la Historia," Manuscript in Nahuatl Language, Library of Congress, Washington, D.C.

Cantares Mexicanos, Poems collected between 1532 and 1597. Edit., Peñafiel, 1904. 1906. Nahuatl Language. National Library of Mexico.

Códice Aubin, Poems and Sagas. Editions: Remi Simeon, Paris, 1893; Peñafiel, Mexico, 1906 (partial). Anonymous manuscript. Nahuatl Language. Library of Berlin.

Códice de Cuauhtitlan, 1558. Annals, poems, and sagas. Also named *Leyenda de los Soles.* Editions: Del Paso Troncoso, Florencia, 1903; Lehman, Berlin, 1938.

Códice de Cuauhtitlan, first part, 1570. Annals, poems, and sages. Also named *Codice de Chimalpopoca.* Editions: Lehman, 1938; Velasquez, 1945, University of Mexico, 1945 (fasc.)

Códice Borgia, A pre-Columbian Codex preserved in the Ethnographical Museum of the Vatican, Rome. Published by le Duc de Loubat, Rome, 1898.

Códice Cospi (Bologna), A Pre-Columbian Codex preserved in the Library of the University of Bologna. Published by le Duc de Loubat, Rome, 1898.

Códice Fejervary-Mayer, An old Mexican Picture Manuscript in the Liverpool Free Public Museum. Published by le Duc de Loubat, Paris, 1901.

Códice Florentino, Illustrations for Sahagún's Historia de las Cosas de la Nueva Espana. Published by F. del Paso y Troncoso, vol. 5, Madrid, 1905.

Códice Mendoza, Edited by James Cooper, 3 vol., London, 1938.

Códice Nuttal, Ancient Mexican Codex belonging to Lord Zouche of Haryngworth. Peabody Museum of American Archaeology and Etnology, Cambridge, Mass., 1901.

Códice Ramirez, Historia de los Mexicanos por sus Pinturas. Published by Garcia Icazbalceta, Mexico, 1886.

Códice Vaticanus 3738 (Vatican A) (Copy of Codex Telleriano-Remensis) A Post-Columbian Codex in the Library of Vatican, Rome. Published by le Duc de Loubat, Rome, 1900.

Códice Vaticanus 3773 (Vaticanus B). A Pre-Columbian Codex in the Library of Vatican. Published by le Duc de Loubat, Rome, 1896.

Historia Tolteco-Chichimeca, Poems in a manuscript Nahuatl of anonymous author. Published by K. T. Preuss and E. Menguin. First part, 1937; second part, 1938. Baesler Archiv, Beheft 9, Berlin.

Ritos, Fiestas y Ceremonias. Calendario, Historia Azteca. Father Duran's works. Edit. 1867 and 1890. Manuscript in the National Library, Madrid.

Huehuetlatolli, Father Andres de Olmos (work 1547). Nahuatl language. Manuscript in the Library of Congress, Washington, D.C.

Sahagun's Informants (Informantes de Sahagun). Manuscript in Nahuatl language. Edited by F. del Paso y Troncoso, 1905, 1906, 1907, Madrid.

III

INCAN

LITERATURE

(Quechuan Language)

"Letters (litteree) not having existed or their secret being still unknown, we cannot technically speak about 'prehispanic literature'. Nevertheless, it existed, although for the present it falls within the orbit of folklore".[50] The author balances his judgment quite well by giving a reply that affirms on one side the existence of the aboriginal literatures, and on the other makes the qualification as to the proper use of the word literature, be it so because letters were non-existent, or because its code is still unknown. In another section of the same book, referring to writing, he makes another declaration "there is the possibility that in the near future there will be produced in this field a discovery as formidable as that of the Egyptologists and Assyriologists of the past century, with respect to the writing of said regions."[51]

Another author, the already mentioned Henestroza, is more categorical when, referring to the indigenous literature, he declares: "Menendez y Pelayo denied its existence in 1892, and some historians of Mexican literature forget about it when they are not busy belittling it, or treating it with contempt. Their histories always start saying that Mexican literature is only a branch of the Spanish because it is written in Spanish. They consider literature only in its grammatical connotation, in its sense of letters, and affirm that inasmuch as the Indians did not have an alphabet, they did not possess a literature. However, we know that people can be illiterate and, nevertheless, possess a great literature".[52]

The value and existence of the aboriginal literatures—following the conventional use of the word—is gaining, however, in its acknowledgment by the new generation of critics and historians. The Aztec poetry, the Quechuan drama, the Mayan narrations, are being definitely incorporated in Indo-American literature with its historical import, its cultural legacy, and its high aesthetic quality. The same thing does not happen, in general, with writing. And even if there is practically no discussion about the reality of a Mayan writing or about the existence of a graphic communication system among the Aztecs, when the time comes to argue about the Incan Empire, it is customary to deny emphatically their possession of any form of writing. From some Chroniclers of the Indies to Prescott and Von Hagen, the following statement has been continuously repeated: "The Incas had no form of writing".[53] But this fact has not yet been elucidated and other authors not only suspect, but also affirm, the existence of an Incan writing, maintaining that only a code is missing to decipher it.

It appears inconceivable, really, that the men of the Tahuantinsuyo could not have been capable to invent a technique to fix and transmit their thought, seeing that they were actual creators in other fields of human endeavor. There are testimonial documents and many logical ones to maintain our belief that there existed an incipient or evolved Incan writing, perhaps unknown by the people like in the Orient, but whose code has not yet been found. The fact of having remained un-deciphered should not lead us to assume an unjust stand, like that of those who denied systematically the existence of the Egyptian or Chaldean-Assyrian writing, prior to its discovery by Champollion and Oppert.

The favorable thesis of the existence of an Incan writing is main-tained and supported by a series of proven facts:

1. The finding of pictographs, petroglyphs, signs, and drawings on stones, paintings, ceramics, and walls that have all the appearance of hieroglyphics.

2. The existence of *quipus* and *quillcas* for accountability and registry of important events, possible exponents of ideographic writing.

3. The functioning of the Council of the Twelve Old Men—a sort of Supreme Court of Justice—whose administration must have been based on a code to issue verdicts or judgment in accordance with written and compiled laws.

4. The universal use of the *runasimi*: a rich, flexible and evolved language, used as a civilizing instrument and as a political weapon of expansion and unification.

5. The existence itself of the words *quillca* (drawing and paint-ings on cloth, boards or leaves, according to Sarmiento de Gamboa), and *poquecancha* (library).

6. The reiterated asseveration of the principal Chroniclers of the Indies that there was a "special writing" for the registry of the great romances and exploits, the laws and the songs.

Some authors have been spreading the idea that the quipus formed the only system of writing invented by the Incas. "The quipus were not only a nemotechnic aid: it contained a complete writing. And who would doubt that knots, small knots and tied strands of thread can be as capable as our orthographical signs of a perfect phonetic equivalent?"[54] But the quipus, against this and other hasty generalizations, was only an instrument to fix and record the statistical movement of the empire. It constitutes a magnificent and original creation (because the Aztec and Iroquois wampum cannot stand com-parison with this means of nearly perfect accounting), but its use needed the contribution of the *quipucamayoc,* and it is not probable that it could be used to register facts, narratives and songs. Its study, however, has not yet been completed, and in spite of the fact that new and unknown types continue to be found (like No. 3955 at the Regional Museum of Ica, with the novelty of a chromatic gamut of eleven colors), we still miss the code that was taken to the grave by the last decoders (quipucamayocs).

The studies made by Professor Lelan L. Locke, Erland Nordens-kiold and others, have established the numerical value of the knots,

58

and in accordance with their conclusions, the knots represent units, tenths, hundredths, and thousands, according to the height of their location on the string. It remains to investigate the chromatic symbolism, the significance of the colors, that in some quipus may coincide with what Garcilaso noted: (white—silver; yellow—gold; blue—religion; crimson—king; red—man), but whose gamut changes and renews itself to the surprise of the investigators, like in the quipus previously mentioned found and studied by Mexia Kespe in the Regional Museum of Ica (Perú).

We cannot, therefore, base a thesis about the existence of a cordographic writing on the quipus (with phonetic equivalent as Capdevila says, or a complete writing system in itself like Raymund de Sangro believed, affirming besides, that the Incan quipus was superior to the European phonetic writing). At best, apart from its primordial function as a system of accounting, it could have served as a nemotechnical aid to record the chronology of the historical events. And even in this case, it would have been only a mere element of nemotechnical aid, a reminder of the first efforts for the communication of thought, and the testimonial and logical documents prove that the ancient Peruvians knew the pictorial or ornamental stage of writing, and reached also the symbolic or ideographic.

It is no longer a mere narrative of the Chroniclers, or a doubtful oral transmission, but a historically proven fact, of the finding of pictographs in stones of Yonan, Salvati, Chavin, on the rocks of the Jequetepeque River, of those of the Rio Grande in Nazca and in Coaque Island. In 1937 Dr. Julio C. Tello discovered the Pre-Incan temple of Sechin, in Casma Valley, and in the stones which decorate the millenarian temple he found 96 figures and many signs that, judging by their appearance, are ideograms or symbols of a true system of writing.[55] What attracted Tello's attention—the best known Peruvian archaeologist—was a type of complex and eskeuform figures of undoubted ideographic significance.

The historian Luis Valcárcel believes that the thread of a hieroglyphic writing can be traced in the ceremonial vases of the *Keros*, and in the Incan fabrics. The same author affirms that in the Museum of the University of Cuzco there exists a valuable Incan cloth with 88 different signs, which can constitute an alphabet or serve as a base for the reconstruction of an alphabet. This opinion deserves credit if we remember that, in the Chronicles of the Indies, there are not only allusions, but statements about the existence of a graphic medium to transmit or communicate thought. When Viceroy Toledo collected the History of the Incas, he made the affirmers swear to the truth of their narratives "In view of which each and every one of them stated that *everything that is written and painted on the said four cloths*, both in the mummies of the Incas and the medals of their elders, and ayllus and the histories of the valances, was and is the truth".[56]

Toledo himself stated in his letter to the King of Spain "with the one that I wrote from Yucay Valley I send the sample of the tracing of the family tree and geneology of the origin of the Ingas (Incas), who were the tyrants of these kingdoms, with proof of the investigations I had been conducting about this business . . . I promised to send this proof with the history and duly authenticated, together with the authorized cloths of the painting that are now being sent".[57]

The chronicler Montesinos made more surprising revelations when speaking about the succession of the Incan rulers: '. . . He was succeeded by Toca Corca Apu Capac who founded a famous 'University' in Cuzco . . ." "in his time, according to the sayings of the Indians, there were letters and characters in parchment and tree leaves, until everything was lost in about four hundred years. . . . Tupac Cauti ordered, under penalty of death, that no one should use quillcas or certain tree leaves on which they wrote".[58]

The origin of the prohibition, according to the same chronicler, could have been due to the reply of the God Illacta Huira Cocha to Tupac Cauri's consultation about the plague that fell upon the empire: "one reply was to the effect that the *cause of the plague had been the letters and that* no one should use them or resurrect them". This is somewhat strange information which takes a naive turn with the addition that "this oracle is kept with such faith that the Peruvians never used letters; and because sometime later a wise *amauta* invented some characters, he was burned alive. From that time on they used cords—quipus."[59] This frank hypothesis about the disappearance of writing in obedience to an oracle is hardly admissible, but perhaps in it we can get a handhold on the suspicion that the first conquerors knowingly destroyed the testimony of the Incan writing, and spread the version that it did not exist or could not find it because of its destruction by its own inventors, following the orders of the gods.

The suspicion is not venturesome if we remember the fate that befell the Mayan and Aztec documents of their writing, and the blind and systematic destruction of everything that could revive in the Indians "the multitude of memories from their past". For the conquerors—I refer to the first brood of soldiers and priests specially—Indian meant infidel, and infidel meant *savage*, and to say infidel and savage was synonymous with *beast* and *enemy*. If "killing infidels was a holy cause", per a well-known motto of the invaders, it could have been quite natural to annihilate everything that the various generations of infidels had created and perpetuated, across a many times millenarian history. The brutal destruction of a cultural conquest like writing—one of the signs of civilization that brought natives and invaders to a level of equality—must have been, just for this reason, particularly tenacious.

We owe to these facts that until now it has not been possible to undertake a thorough study of the culture of the Tahuantinsuyo and the Pre-Incan cultures. The studies about the South-American past, lacking written sources of information, have been resigned to the utilization of archaeological monuments, the grammars of the Quechua, folklore, the itineraries of the parish priests, the version of the Chroniclers of the Indies, the oral tradition transmitted by Amautas, Villac-umas and surviving nobles. We must remember in this respect that though Indian history was received orally by the chroniclers (and transmitted to them with the assistance of memory, quipus, and according to some of cloths and painted fabrics), it has been fully corroborated by the scientific studies undertaken on textiles, ceramics, archaeological monuments, surviving indigenous tongues; that is to say, with the assistance of technical studies and verification of testimonies offered by art, science and aboriginal linguistics.

Thus a partial reconstruction of the past of the Incan Empire has been possible. And though parcelled and defective insofar as it applies to their cultural life, it reveals to us the existence of poetry, drama and narrative, as logical manifestations of the great creative spirit of our aboriginal ancestors. There was, therefore, a true "Incan literature" even though the term literature appears improper for the present. We shall continue to employ this term with the reservation that we do not use it in its literal significance, but as a denominator of the whole of the creative expressions—written or unwritten—of the sensibility and thought of a people.

OFFICIAL LITERATURE AND POPULAR LITERATURE

The Incan Empire "was a superposition of agricultural communities, the result of a long evolution, by the side of a State socialism created by men".[60] The agrarian collectivism of the economy and the type of theocratic-imperial government are manifested clearly in their literature, as well as in the other cultural expressions of the Incan civilization.

The political autocratism—of paternalistic appearance, divine origin and social aims—gave way to courtlike literature, official, "directed", which had in its charge the romances, the imperial chronicles, the cult hymnals, the dramas and the comedies, the social poems, the educational theatre, the moralizing stories, and the philosophical counsels. The agrarian socialism inspired a spontaneous literature, popular, lyric, intimately joined with nature.

It is possible to talk about another literature: the one born as a result of malaise, pain or protest, both from the *mitimaes* and from those who resented the practices of the Empire, which annoyed and opposed the free expression of sensibility. This literature flourished in some *Urpis*-lyric of longing, painful disenchantment, penetrating nos-

61

talgia—it comes to light in the fables—an allusive form of rebellion and vengeance—and reaches the themes of clandestine epic.

THE AUTHORS

Amautas and *Haravicus* were the creators of this literature. The Amautas—also counsellors, historians and philosophers—were the authors of epic poetry and the theater. As poets and functionaries attached to the court, they composed the great commemorative poems to celebrate and exalt all events of political and social import—war victories, enthronement of the emperors, rich harvests, arrival of the rains, beginning of campaigns, blooming of the fields. They were in charge of the chronicle of the imperial history and had the special mission of preserving and spreading tradition. They were also authors of the invocational and thanksgiving hymns to the guardian gods. Their influence in the direction of culture was not limited to the Yachayhuasi, they were the instructors and counsellors of nobility, during youth and the exercise of power, and to them is attributed the creation of the Moral Code and the philosophical guides that ruled human and social life.

The Haravicus were the popular poets, creators of the lyric "which some times declaimed extemporaneous verses chorused by the multitude", and who helped the Amautas in the composition of the collective epic and lyric songs. They were the authors of a soft, amatory poetry, of a minor tone, fresh and flowering, part of which turns pathetic and vibrant when the anguish that moves the uprooted heart of the mitimaes intervenes with its new emotion. The Haravicus created, besides, a gay and agile poetry in the *cashuas*; solemn and pantheistic in the *wancas*; with willful gaiety, sometimes frantic, in the rural *aymorays*; exalted, martial, dionysiac for the *haylles*; tender and picaresque for the wayno.

Haravicus is the Quechuan term for naming the poets and means inventors, creators. The Haravicus compose harawis, that is, inventions, poetic creations. Harawi must have been, therefore, the generic word to designate the lyric poetry, and for the types, the other denominations: urpi, haylli, wanca, aymoray. The poets invented harawis that could be told, sung, and enacted.

The majority of the lyric poetry known to date comes joined to the music and the dance. From that arises its predominant rhythmic character. There were exceptions, probably, corresponding to the declamation in the epic, ritual poetry and, perhaps, to the subjective poetry of the mitimaes. In general, the dance inspires the rhythm of the music and this in turn transmits it to the verse imposing its meter. Therefore we can speak of an art of metrical composition. At the beginning the *hararec* was utilized, a meter in consonance with the initial pentatonic scale of music; to the later musical evolution a more ample versification belonged afterwards, because "the poets of the Empire learned to compose short and long verses", but they "did not know consonance. All verses were free".[61]

This last part of Garcilaso's quotation is contradicted by many samples of Incan poetry. The urpis of the Ollantay have a regular rhythm. There are other poems, however, where the consonance is irregular or does not exist. It is useless to try to judge the poetry of the Empire with the rules of the occidental literary preceptive. For Amautas and Haravicus it appears that no fundamental preoccupation ever existed for meter and rhythm. Jesús Lara believes that in the meter, "more so than in the number of syllables, was the tonic structure of the words taken into consideration", and that the rhythm was formed without deliberate effort, by reason of the nature of the language which possesses an astounding profusion of words with the same endings, and due to factors derived from the idiomatic characteristics of the quechua (lack of article, special formation of the pronoun, and a typical verbal conjugation).

Generally, the verses of the Incan poetry do not go over ten syllables. The most popular have five syllables, but there are many with four syllables, six syllables and even eight syllables. Tetrasyllabic and trisyllabic combinations are found, also decasyllabic, pentasyllabic, and of six and two syllables.

Poetry, music and the dance had uniform expressions for particular feasts and collective ceremonies, but were differentiated, logically, under the influence of the geography, the nature of the work, temperament, customs, and the language of the four regions of the Empire (Antisuyo, Collasuyo, Contisuyo and Chinchasuyo).

Apart from the erotic song of the llactaruna and the nostalgic lyric of the mitimaes, all Incan poetry was earmarked for collective use. It was recited or sung in the open air, in front of nature, before human concentrations. The groups or multitudes confined themselves to listen on occasions; at other times they joined in chorus, now with simple stimulating interjections, now intoning chants, in popular singing choruses that have not been repeated in later history.

Alone, or accompanied by music and dance, poetry is very evident in all signal events of the imperial life: in the great taquis, agricultural labors, funeral ceremonies, collective tasks, and official holidays of the Incan calendar. It was closely tied to the customs, religion, work, politics, and culture. Like the theater, it performed a social function. For this reason it represents one of the best clues to know and interpret the entire life of the empire of the Incas.

THE TYPES OF THE LYRIC

Among the examples of poetry that the oral tradition has transmitted, that the quechuists have restored, or the Chroniclers of the

Indies have related, we note the frequent use of the dialogue. It is a dialogized lyric that appears indistinctively in poems of rural, religious, and sentimental inspiration.

There is an individual who leads the singing, and the group choruses the replies. The leader sings or recites the principal verses, the rest reply with an exclamation, a special refrain, or the last foot of the stanza. They were the songs "wherein all sang at once, the rest intoning and following".[62] "The most common practice is for all to sing, one or two reciting their poetry, the rest assisting in the response with the foot of the stanza".[63]

A typical example of this dialogized poetry would be the *wawaki*, sung by juvenile choruses of both sexes during the lunar feasts or during the night watches to guard the sown fields. Let us look at an example:

1. The Youths
   Because you are a star
   You shine at night
       Yes!
   I look for you in vain
   In the daytime.
       Yes!

2. The Young Girls
   If I am a star
   Open your heart;
   Turn your eyes
   Under the sunlight.

3. The Youths
   You make believe you call me
   only in the moonlight
       Yes!
   But when I come near
   You are like the snow
       Yes!

4. The Young Girls
   If I feign to call you
   Come quickly;
   If I seem like the snow,
   Give me your fire.

5. The Youths
   When my fire burns you
   You turn into dew
       Yes!
   Are you perhaps like a frenzy
   Or only an illusion?
       Yes?

6. The Young Girls
   If you think I am dew
   Bring up your lips
       Yes!
   Even if it's only an illusion,
   Don't lose sight of me.
       No!

(From the *Collection of Mendez-Bolivia*—Free translation.)

The contradictory notes from the chroniclers, and the confusion or change of names in the oral tradition, do not allow the preparation of a complete classification of the different types achieved by the Incan lyric poetry. By making a study of the verses known to date, a classification can be attempted, noting the following main varieties: Aymoray, haylle, urpi, cashua, wanka and wayno.

THE AYMORAY, an agile, gay poetry, of rural inspiration, currently uses the dialogue. It sings to the trees, dialogues with the rain and the winds, invokes the blessing of the Gods, exalts the mission of water for irrigation, celebrates farm labors. The canto of the aymoray seems to have been the *ayrihuay*, intoned during the season of the harvest of the grain in the *pirwas*, and the *ayrihuaymito* the dance or one of the dances held during the corn festivals.

The aymoray most mentioned by the chroniclers[64] are those sung during the month of May, when the Indians "celebrated a feast from the sown fields to their homes, singing, dancing and beseeching the idols to protect their food".[65]

WARIJSA ARAWI

The men
The song, the song!
Not the song of sadness
But the song of gaiety.

The women
The song, the song!

The men
With elegance, yes, with elegance!
How I love elegance!
With elegance!

The women
With elegance, yes, with elegance!

The men
Do you have "aji" in your field?
I shall come using it as a pretext
Are there flowers in your garden?
I shall pretend I come for them.

A man:
Behold the queen!

The women
Wipha, yes, that is the queen!
Wipha, there she is!
Wipha, yes, that is the ñusta!
Wipha, yes, that's she!

YARKAPAC (To an irrigation canal)

Long and beautiful canal
Whose smooth breast
Shall carry the water to our sown fields.
Dance!

Let us dance energetically
Dance!
Tread forcefully
Dance!

65

Because of you
the plants will flower
Dance!
The wonderful fruit
shall multiply
Dance!

Let us dance energetically
Dance!
Tread forcefully
Dance!

RURAL AYMORAY

1.—*Shower, little shower,*
  Please don't wet me
  For my poncho is short.

—*Hail, little hail,*
  Please don't fall on me,
  For my poncho is thin.

—*Wild wind, little wild wind,*
  Do not blow on me,
  For I am in rags.

Fun, fun,
  Let us have fun!
  I would even step on the thorns!
  I would even step on the stones!

2.—*Ah, ha, ha, ha, little shepherdess,*
  You go to the hill
  And the cóndor hovers.

—*Ah, ha, ha, ha, little shepherd*
  You go to the mount
  And the hawk flies and flies.

—*Ah, ha, ha, ha, shepherds*
  You climb to the pirca,
  And the fox follows the scent.

(From *"Quechuan White Lilies"*—Recopilation of Unos Parias—Lima, 1905).

THE HAYLLE, which means literally "triumph", has been well named the song of labor and victory. Martial and dionysiac, of a rural or heroic theme, always enthusiastic, vigorous, euphoric, the haylle is the highest expression of collective hope and happiness. It records the imperial victories, interprets the joyous gratitude of the people towards the beneficent gods, express the virile passion of labor and the tense rejoicing of man before the lavish reward of the land. For that reason it has as many varieties as the states of mind it expresses.

MALQUIPAC (To the plant)
    (Rural Haylle)

> Beautiful plant, luxuriant tree,
> whose shade sheltered me.
>   haylle!
>
> You opened your arms
> To our generation.
>   haylle!
>
> Haylle, lovely plant.
>   haylle!

(*Quechuan grammar* of José Dionisio Anchorena. Lima, Perú, 1874).

TIJSI VIRACOCHA
    (Sacred Haylle)

> God, origin of the Universe,
> Creator of all.
> Gold that burns only
> In the bottom of the heart.
> May the gaiety of your eyes
> arrive with the dawn!
> May the warmth of your breath
> come with the wind!
> May your magnanimous hand
> always be extended,
> And may your eternal will
> be the only one that flowers.

AYAU HAYLLE
    (Agricultural Haylle)

> The men:
> *Hey, haylle! Hey, haylle!*
> *Here is the plow and the furrow!*
>
> The women:
> *Wipha, man, wipha!*
>
> The men:
> *Hey, haylle! Hey, haylle!*
> *Where is the beautiful ñusta?*
> *Where is the seed, where is the furrow?*
>
> The women:
> *Wipha, the seed, wipha!*
>
> The men:
> *Hey, haylle! Hey, haylle!*
> *Powerful sun, our father,*
> *Give me your breath, bless the furrow!*

The women:
Wipha, Father Sun, Wipha!

The men.
Hey, haylle! Hey, haylle!
Oh, womb of Pachamama
that gives life and fertilizes!

The women:
Wipha, Pachamama, wipha!

The men:
Hey, haylle! Hey, haylle!

The women:
Wipha! Wipha!

(From *Mendez Collection*, Bolivia.)

AYAU JAILLINIÑA! (Hey, I have conquered!)

The men:
Wipha! Wipha!
I have sown the grain.

The women:
Haylle! Haylle!

The men:
The plant will grow
I shall care for it.

The women:
Haylle! Haylle!

The men:
The rain shall come,
Its waters shall fall.

The women:
Haylle! Haylle!

The men:
And the flowers shall come,
The fruits shall come forth.

The women:
Haylle! Haylle!

The men:
The sun rains gold
And the moon rains silver.

The women:
Haylle! Haylle!

The men:
I sowed the seed
I planted the food.

68

The women:
Haylle! Haylle!

(From *Vasquez Collection*, Bolivia).

The URPI. Sometimes, improperly, the name *harawi* is given to this variety of the Incan lyric poetry. We have already stated that *harawi* must be used like a synonym of the poetical creation, inasmuch as it is the word from which the derivation has come to name the "inventors of poetry" or *haravicus*.

The *harawis* were gay and "even dionysiac" in the Empire.[66] They were also "songs in the manner of dirges"[67] or "songs of the deeds of others or remembrance of loved ones."[68] "They recalled past events"[69] or "they told about the Inca and sang his praises."[70]

All these lyrical effusions received the general name of *harawis*. They were not limited to amatory poetry. The sentimental *harawi*, the sad song that recalled the deeds of the absent lovers, has been the poetic and musical root of the current mixed song which adopted as its name the same modified word of *yaraví*, giving birth to the belief that the *harawi* was the sad and sentimental song of the Empire, and pretending to take away from the vocable its generic denominating category.

The erotic *harawi*, the lyric of the quechuan lover, the romantic poetry of the empire, is in the *urpis*. They are songs of fluid verses, of soft cadence, free rhythm and clean melodic line. Definitive studies about its meter are lacking. Studying the known *urpis*, we can distinguish a regular meter of equal number of accents and syllables, and an irregular form which does not consider the number of syllables, and is constructed from a base of constant accents in number, but not in placement.

The *urpi* runs over all the themes of the amatory lyric. Disillusionment, longing, indifference, and hope, manage to bring their romantic messages to this poetry of fresh, allegorical and emotive language. It appears flowing in its bucolic or pastoral version. Ordinarily, the emotion of the amorous lament—stoic, downcast, or imploring—gives to the verse an intense vibration. Sometimes it twitches with the recondite clamors of nostalgia or hopelessness, and also resorts to the pathetic means of imprecation. This expression, which partakes of the "saudade" and expresses a sort of desolate anguish, does not seem like the expression of the lover *llactaruna*— the native lover—but an effusion of the *mitimae*, whose exiled heart bears equally the tortures of love and the longing for the distant fatherland.

There are brief and compendious *urpis* of a surprising conciseness. Like the Japanese *haikais*, they condense in a few lines a whole poetic discourse.

THE LOST DOVE

—*"Where are you my dove?*
I search for you day and night.
Perhaps you are crying
Lost amid a distant jalca
Not knowing how to return . . ."
I ask everyone
Perhaps I shall find her trail
And run to find her.
Where are you, my dove?
I have searched for you a year and a day.

PASTORAL

I would like a llama
With golden hairs
Brilliant like the sun
Strong as love,
Soft like the cloud
Dissolved by the dawn.
I would then make a quipus
Where I could record
The flowers that die . . .
The passing clouds. . . .

(Song of Cuzco—Recopilation of Alomías Robles).

TAQUI

You are a beautiful flower,
I am a sharp thorn;
You are happiness made life,
I am increasing sadness.
A white cloud, the lightest one,
A sweet fountain of pure water,
You shall be my sweet deceit,
I shall be your dark shadow.

(Taqui fragment—Anthology of Farfan).

TAPUCITO L'LATA

Where does my treasure hide?
At midnight I cry for her
I miss her every hour.

(E. & D. D'Harcourt. Incan Music and its Survivances. Paris, 1825).

Other *urpis* are of greater extension, but they do not lose their poetic density. In the following examples one becomes aware of the greatest expressive agility reached by the verses with the animation of the most elaborate metaphors.

ABSENT

Doesn't your heart pain you?
Don't you cry over it,
Being my Coya,
Being my Ñusta?
I remember your liclla and cry.
I remember your ajsu and suffer.
No day comes after my night,
there is no dawn for my sky.
For you I live a prisoner,
If sorrow shall destroy me,
I shall end in oblivion,
You, my Coya,
You, my love
Don't you remember me?

HARAY HARAWI

Haray, harawi,
What fate persecutes us?
What barriers separate us?
Darling ciclla, chinchircoma flower,
You are in my heart,
I carry you within my thought.
We are apart because of your mother
and your father.
We suffer because we cannot see each other.
I turn mad with grief remembering your eyes,
I am ill remembering your lovely glances.

Who knows, my ñusta, if the sun will join us someday?
And perhaps will to join us forever!
It is so, Father, I must tell you this way,
If you condemn me to cry,
Why don't you have pity on me?

Crying over the road
Over the kantutas,
through the sad valley
I wait, however, for my lovely ciclla.

(Version of the urpis taken from New Chronicle and Good Government, by Guaman Poma de Ayala).

The CASHUA, which continues to exist somewhat changed, was the dance of happiness, performed in the squares and fields. Its music has sometimes the rural accent of the aymoray and provokes a contagious gaiety, similar to that of the haylle, but more spontaneous and less solemn.

Here is an example:

> *The time will come to cheer our Inca,*
> *We shall dance for him at the full moon*
> *We shall sing our sweetest song.*
> *The time has come to dance for our Inca.*
> *Meanwhile my tuya, my dove,*
> *I am not afraid of the full moon;*
> *Let us meet in the blooming meadow,*
> *to play with our golden star.*
>
> (From the *Mendez Collection*, Bolivia).

The WAYNO, because of its erotic character, gives the impression of having been the dance of some of the *urpis*. The dance has survived until today and is performed by couples dancing in front of each other, executing flashy movements to the tempo of the *tinyas* and other instruments. Since the Empire, and even today, the lyrics of the wayno have an amorous inspiration deeply allied with nature. Farfan's Anthology has an example of its poetical quality. We cite a fragment:

* * * * * *

> *You carry a robe woven with flowers.*
> *Its woof is made of golden threads.*
> *Its fine fringes are tied with my tenderness.*

* * * * * *

The WANKA is a type of poetry with an invocational character, solemn and profound, saturated with a crude pathos, with a viril and balanced sadness. It is thought that it was some sort of a lyric response, of grand elegy over the death of the loved ones, and of significance in the individual and collective sentiment.

We furnish two examples: one dedicated to a tree with a pleasant and fertile history, and fragments of the one composed to the death of Atahualpa.

WANKA (To a dead tree.)

> *Protective shadow, a way of life,*
> *You were.*
>
> *Within your foliage my heart nested;*
> *My happiness blossomed beneath your shade.*
>
> *Is it possible that you depart alone?*
> *Will you never open your eyes again?*
> *Which way will you go leaving me behind,*
> *Never opening your flowers again?*
> *What tree will now give me its shade?*
> *What foliage shall give me its song?*
> *How can I remain so alone?*
>
> *The world shall be a desert without you,*
>
> (From the *Vásquez Collection*, Bolivia. Free translation).

72

APU INCA ATAHUALPAMAN (To the great Inca Atahualpa).

What nefarious rainbow is this black rainbow that rises?
The foe throws a horrible dart,
A sinister hail spreads everywhere.

* * * * * *

Atahualpa's great heart
Has become cold.
All the Tahuantinsuyo is now sobbing.

* * * * * *

Bloody tears torn from departed happiness,
Picture his corpse in your mirror,
And bathe with your tenderness
The lap of him who bestowed us kindness
With his many hands,
And sheltered us beneath his heart,
And covered us with the shade of his breast.

* * * * * *

Our father,
The blood is clotted in your veins.
Your sight is faded,
Your glance is perhaps in the light of a star.
Will your heart allow,
O sovereign King
That we should live dispersed and wandering,
Subjugated and downtrodden by an alien power?
Let us discover your eyes that know how to enlighten
With their rays of kindness.
Extend your hand to us,
That hand that bestows more than we ask for.
And comforted with that boon,
Tell us to leave!

(From *Quechua Folkloric Poetry*—JMB Farfan).

The following fragments seem to be also from a Wanka:

THE CRY OF THE ÑUSTAS

Let us cry
Tears of blood
Let us cry.

With desperation, aloud!
Let us cry.

We will not see his eyes again,
We will not hear his voice again,
Let us cry!

73

No longer his kind look
Shall gaze over his people.
Let us cry!

With tears of blood,
Let us cry!

(From *"Cantares Quechuas"*—D. Alomías Robles).

RITUAL POETRY

In the literature of the Empire we find a style of poetry dedicated to worship, whose evolution is notable. Besides the sacred haylles there are hymns, invocations, and praises which possess a powerful mystical spirit and reveal a high conception of divinity. The mysticism of this poetry sometimes contains an erotic accent or sometimes adorns itself with a lovely malice. Both characteristics can be observed in the beautiful ballad transmitted to us by Garcilaso. It was dedicated to the beneficent rain and holds close analogy with those vedic hymns in which the atmospheric agents are personified, and Nature's phenomena are given life.

But without doubt, the hymn of greatest literary merit and more advanced religious conception is the one transcribed below. As an example, it is most eloquent to demonstrate that the Incan religion had already recast its anthropomorphic myths into a real abstract monotheism. It faithfully represents the longing towards a mystical and intimate communion with the Eternal Principle. By the distressed clamor of its doubts expressed in questionings and pathetic apostrophes to the Unknown Creator, it can be compared to the Hymn of Creation of the Rig Veda. There is nothing like it in the biblical psalms. Besides, the Incan hymn does not interpret the tortures of a single mind or an individual state of mind: it is the interpretation of the collective mystical feeling, of the tense and vibrant religious restlessness of the empire, through the philosophical meditations of the Amautas:

Oh, Viracocha, Lord of the Universe,
Male or female
You that engender and conceive,
I anxiously conjure thee!

Am I not your son?
Where are you hiding?

In the sublime immensity where you dwell
Within the depths of the sea where you reside,
O, creator of the world
O, creator of man,
Supreme Lord,
My sight grows faint trying to see you.

74

If I could know you,
Contemplate you,
Understand you
You would also see me
And shelter me.

The sun, the moon, the day, the night,
The ocean and the universe,
Obediently set out towards their goals;
No matter what it is,
It shall reach the end
Designated by your scepter.

Inspire me! Help me!
I call upon you with all the strength of my voice.
Hear me! Choose me!
Don't let me faint, don't let me die!

Oh! Viracocha!
If I could be allowed to see you!
If I could be allowed to know you!
If I could be allowed to understand you!

(Free version of the text of *Alejandro Korn. Vida Nueva.* Buenos Aires, 1922.
Original text published by Ximenez de la Espada, España).

THE EPIC LITERATURE

The first expressions of the Incan Epic give a glimmering explanation of the creation of the world and its beings. They are the theogonic and cosmogonic initial themes. Myths, legends, ballads, express the collective beliefs from the era of the *purumpacha* (uninhabited time, vacuum) until the legendary appearance of the founders of nations and dynasties. Religion appears, confusing its origins with those of the infantile epic.

Two legends are worth citing as examples of this fabulous epic: that of Viracocha, which refers to the creation of the world; and that of the Ayar brothers, the heroes of the founding of the empire.

Harmonizing the version of the chroniclers Santa Cruz Pachacuti, Juan de Dios Betanzos, Pedro Sarmiento de Gamboa, a condensed and complete text can be obtained of the impressive legend of Viracocha, a God that appeared when there were not light nor fire, during Chaos, creating a dark world and giants of stone, and later, over the destruction of these first beings that sinned, bringing forth a new world with light under whose brilliance he peoples the earth with more perfect beings. His task finished, Viracocha, accompanied by his assistants, crosses rivers, valleys, mountains, issuing forth the magic words that order the new stone beings to live, multiply and fill the earth. From different roads, finally, the God and his assistants meet on the seashore and disappear beyond the sea, walking on it without sinking. Because the God walked over the waves without sinking, or like the sea foam, they called him Viracocha.

According to other legends Viracocha was born from Chaos, created the world and fought with numerous rebels. He did all this and even created the form and archtype of early humanity, but did not properly create man. Afterwards the God Con arrived "he who appeared from the North and had no bones" (Lopes de Gómara). This God of the Rain would also create men without bones. He walked for long distances and rapidly, "he shortened the road, lowered the mountains, raised the valleys, all this at his will and with words". "But, due to evil done to him, he turned the good earth he had bestowed on them into dry and sterile deserts. He took away the rain. Out of his mercy, he left them only the rivers so they could till the earth with irrigation and toil" (this legend alludes to the aspect of the Peruvian coastline, arid, dry without real rain, cut from place to place by rivers flowing down from the Andes to provide irrigation to the land). Con's wrath ruined the world, but after him came Pachacamac, the God that maintains the life of the Universe. "He created men and women as they are today, and provided them with everything they have".

The legend of the Ayar brothers is very well known and belongs to more recent times. According to it, four brothers and their respective wives, and legions descended from Viracocha, departed with their people from the windows of Tamputoco (the Inn of the windows) with the divine mission to found an empire. The valley of Cuzco (the world's navel) was reached only by the women and two of the brothers, Ayar Manco and Ayar Ochu, because the rest had perished on the road. Ayar Ochu was turned into stone when he took possession of the place. Ayar Manco, the survivor who bore the *tupayauri* (a wand with inscriptions given by Viracocha) accomplished the God's mandate. Under his command the pilgrims conquered the resistance of the valley's inhabitants and founded the overlordship of the Sons of the Sun, the first cell of the future confederacy of the Tahuantisuyo. The legend, related by the majority of the chroniclers, reveals the historical myth of Manco Capac, founder of the empire, and the Ayar Manco of the fabulous narration.

THE EPIC OF THE AMAUTAS

The official literature, courtlike, directed, had a special chapter dedicated to fix and perpetuate the epic poems of the empire and the heroic biographies of the emperors. In this epic, written by command and under the supervision of the monarchs, the worry of the Incas about the future is patently revealed, as well as in the funeral *huacas*, the cyclopean constructions, and the educative projection of the literature. The epic assumed the responsibility of faithfully translating that powerful will to survive in the hymns, ballads, narratives that were definitely incorporated into the official tradition of the empire. The epic poems were recited or sung in solemn occasions, during the great commemorations of the Incan calendar, with the triple purpose of exalting the glorious deeds, inspire the national pride of the people, and stimulate the spirit of the spectators to emulate the heroic deeds.

To fix the imperial tradition different procedures were followed: the simple events were registered in the *quipus* and the memorable events in the *quillcas*. Quipus and quillcas formed the archives which were maintained and kept in the *poque-canchas* (libraries). But these means were not enough because there were details that could not or were not convenient to record on quipus or quillcas; then the quipucamayoc of records were resorted to. (The quipucamayoc was a sort of scribe of the quechuas, in charge of statistics, accountability and registry of certain historical events).

The tradition having been set up, it had to be spread among the people in a brief, wide and easy manner. The poetic tone, the length of the poems and the complexity of the themes dealt with, were not fitted to the purpose of a sure, easy and faithful transmission of the magnificence of the empire in the memories of the generations. The Amautas, therefore, translated into the prose the long poems and condensed their contents in "historical stories, brief, like fables, to be told to children, young and peasants, according to their ages" (Garcilaso de la Vega). Garcilaso himself speaks about the collaboration of the haravicus in this synthesis of historical events when he says that "they prepared brief and condensed verses" in which they covered "the history, or commission or reply of the King".

The most famous epic ballad is the one dedicated to the Inca Pachacutec, a sovereign who governed the Tahuantisuyo when the splendor of the imperial unification was initiated. The long argument of the poem, recognized and praised by practically all the chroniclers, appears as an uneven text, but with identical base, in the works of Betanzos, Sarmiento de Gamboa and Santa Cruz Pachacuti.

THE EPIC OF RESISTANCE.

If some of the urpis surreptitiously expressed the nostalgia of the mitimaes, and the resentment of those who suppressed their feelings about the prohibitions of the Incan legislation, the epic collected the clandestine ballads narrating deeds of the resistance or the rebellion against the empire.

The history of the empire of the Incas reveals to us the vast enterprise accomplished by its sovereigns. The task of conquering and incorporating hundreds of peoples as active cells within the Great Empire was not an easy one. The struggle was extensive and filled with vicissitudes. And after it came the campaign, no less arduous, of consolidating the conquests. The war, one way or the other, provided the heroic material for the official epic, and nourished the series of ballads that would be perpetuated by popular memory among the conquered peoples.

When Lcdo. Polo de Ondegardo speaks about the quipus, he states that "every province has its registers of the victories, wars and punishments of their country". These punishments are none other than those applied by the Incas to the "traitors" or to the peoples who insisted in keeping their freedom, after the first cordial commission sent by the conquerors to secure a peaceful surrender. Thus was preserved, officially, the memory of those great journeys of the resistance and the rebellion, so frequently quoted by the chroniclers of the Indies:—the rebellion of the *chancas* under the command of *Ancoallo* and his famous retreat to Chachapoyas "performing such great deeds that they seem like fables" (Garcilaso); the stubborn fight of the *chimús* to free themselves from the vassalage; the revolt of the *pocras;* the uprising of the *collas* with their chief Xipana; the rebellion of Tocay Capac and his *huallacanes;* the romantic insurrection of *Ollanta.*

With authority from the censorship, the quipucamayoc registered the punishments received, furnishing an official, plain account of the events. There were simple narratives or unpolished verse, brief, concrete, that propagated from generation to generation the odyssey of the heroes, and the vicissitudes of the campaigns against the empire and its imperialistic designs. When rancor or protest needed an escape valve, free from censorship and punishment, they would appeal to the suggestive and caustic satire of the fables.

THE THEATER.

The Amautas were not lacking in ability, inasmuch as they were philosophers, to compose comedies and tragedies, which they performed before their kings and lords during the solemn feasts and ceremonies. The performers (actors) were not peasants, but Incas and people of noble blood, sons of chiefs, and captains, and even Masters of the Field (Marshals), because the plot of the tragedies represented reality, and they were always about military deeds, triumphs, and accomplishments, and about the heroic acts and greatness of the late kings and other heroic warriors. The plots of the comedies were about farmers, agriculture, and household affairs. "They never dealt with dishonest things; they dealt with serious and honest affairs, with properties and customs permitted in a particular place." (Garcilaso Inca de la Vega—Royal Commentaries).

That is one of the many references to the Inca theatre. About

78

it and its performances, mainly talk Guaman Poma de Ayala, Villa-gomez, Santa Cruz Pachacuti, Polo, Estete, Betanzos, Molina, Morúa, Fernandez de Oviedo, Cieza de Leon, Arriaga, Cobo, Sarmiento. There abound references and allusions among the Chroniclers of the Indies. The oral tradition, besides, has preserved the plots of various theatrical works—Atahualpa, Ushca Paucar, among others, as well as songs and dances of the ancient representations, that are performed even to this date, with the logical distortions of time, by the descendants of que-chuas and aymaras.

It seems that one of the elemental and typical forms of this theater were the *taquis,* magnificent collective dances performed in the plazas in connection with religious festivities, the beginning of farm work, the starting of campaigns, and commemoration of victories. Dancers with masks and disguises performed complicated choreographic evolu-tions, while the chanting of the ritual hymns and the war songs were chorused by the crowd. The taqui finished involving the multitude in its gaiety and its action.

Guaman Poma de Ayala furnishes direct information about these festivals. "Taqui dances of the Incas and Capac-apoconas and principals and of the common Indians of these kingdoms of the Chinchaysuyos, Andesuyos, Collasuyos, and Condesuyos": "Taqui cahina haylli-araqi, of the lasses—pingollo of the young men—fest of the shepherds—many llamayo, and of the farmers, pachacaharanayo—of the collas, quirquina-collina-aymarana—of the lasses, guanca. . . ." (New Chronicle and Good Government).

RELIGIOUS AND CIVIC THEATRE

The Inca theatre was not limited to these festivals with representa-tions restricted to the dance, the pantomime and the chorus, as in a primitive ballet. Commentaries tell us about a religious theater which had in its cast an idol, a priest and the faithful. The priest questioned the god in the name of the people and transmitted the replies to the audience, who in turn answered with choral expressions of happi-ness or sadness. In their capacity as intermediaries, the priests and the Incas took advantage of these representations to educate the people, under divine inspiration, in the technique and art of certain practices which acquired a surprising similarity and perfection in the empire (the handling of the taclla (plow), the echeloned geometry of the paths, the construction of the aqueducts, the ritual paraphernalia in the planting and harvesting, the conservation and harnessing of water, the opening of canals and development of roads).

Another variety, and more evolved, of the representations, is found in a sort of civic or military theater in which the presence of the priest is merely decorative. A classical example of this theatre would be the *huarachicoy,* in honor of Huari, the god of virility. It was performed during the great feast of *Capac-Raymi* for the purpose of "qualifying the youths" for their entrance or admission in the team of selected citizens, destined for government or military command. The arrival of the youths to the huarachicoy signified the possession of the highest virtues, after a very careful physical and intellectual preparation supervised by the *amautas.* The *amautas* instructed them in the *Yachayhuasi,* in order to assimilate everything relating to history, morals, administrative practices and the ideals of the empire. The huarachicoy was the last test, examination and qualification of their aptitudes, done in the presence of the Incan, the nobles and the people.

The Incas used this theater also to propagate and perpetuate the outstanding events of their biographies, and the memorable happenings of their military history. The plot was based on the exploits of an emperor and the performance was in charge of nobles and supernumeraries, in the presence of the Inca, the people and the mummies of the dead emperors. Sometimes the performance included sham battles, reviving the battle scenes perfectly. Besides their aesthetic finality, this theater was eminently pedagogic, and its performances must have stirred profound emotions in the spectators. The presence of the royal mummies in the scene allowed for the comparison of their achievements with those of the governing Inca, and offered healthy stimuli to the emperor himself to emulate and surpass the glories of his ancestors. Insofar as the people were concerned, the magnificent and enlightening performance of their history, must have incited in them, besides an enthusiastic reaction to their collective pride, the most stimulating desires for individual emulation.

COMIC THEATRE

Dealing with the comic theatre it is supposed it did not achieve great development due to the Inca's majesty and that of the nobles, and to the lack of the proper atmosphere for political satire. But there are other sources of inspiration for the comic theatre, and they were exploited in the empire because we know about the utilization of the parody in fables and comedies. Giving it an educational meaning, it portrayed the characteristics of animals—astuteness, ingenuity and dynamism—in order to create gay arguments and to reproach vices. Lies, robbery, laziness were attacked with the festive instrument given by the burlesque performance of the life of the animals. Furthermore, the chroniclers tell about the existence of "clowns and jokers that some *guacas* had all over the kingdom of Pirú". (Cristobal de Molina, ob. cit.). They were also found in the palaces and their role was similar to that of the buffoons and jugglers of the European courts. Mama Cova, the wife of Capac Yupanqui "had clowns of the Inca, and coarse jokers, like we call among ourselves, very fresh," (Morúa, ob. cit.). If the existence of these personages is assured, why can't we believe in the creation of comedies and farces, theatrical pieces for relaxation, if we have proof of the creative imagination, and the frequency of the feasts for popular enjoyment, as marked in the Incan calendar?

The interesting point is to fix the era when the empire is transformed and a favorable atmosphere is born for the free play of all the expressions of art. In this respect, some authors sustain the belief that Pachacutec was the last absolute representative of the governing castes "of divine origin." The later Incas suffer a sort of "humanization" by virtue of the social forces of the community, which rebel against the omnipotence of the imperial theocracy. The "inflexible primitive hieratism having been broken, the national sentiment breaks forth and so does its expression in art". To the new methods in poetry, in the theater, music, would belong the beginnings of a new sculptural and ornamental sense, like the jovial life, engraved in knives and domestic objects, the gay dynamism in statuettes and huacos, the force of the satire, and other expressions of the sensibility, and great decorative sense of the Peruvian Indian.

The symbolic and effective author of the transformation would be Ollanta, who rebels against "the demi-god king, and against the sidereal order that his empire represents in the Tahuantisuyo". Ollanta, to Ricardo Rojas and Cossio del Pomar, not only represents a mortal in love with a forbidden princess; he represents a race in revolt against the political and religious interests of a class; he incarnates the forces of the earth struggling for their liberation; he is the tellurian hero, the Man of the Earth, the Andi, against the Man of the Sky, the Inca. It is not strange, therefore, that the Incan theater has portrayed with freedom the transcendental odyssey of the romantic Incan general. The complete victory of the great rebellion—a sentimental and political victory of Ollanta—permitted the creation and perpetuation of the drama.

THE OLLANTAY

The Ollantay is an anonymous drama, in the quechuan tongue, whose writing in Spanish characters must have been made during the first years of the conquest. It was discovered by Valdez, a priest, who directed its first performance, it is believed, before Tupac Amaru, the great leader of the revolution of 1780. There exists an oral version of the Indian Fabio Tito and its plot is, more or less given, in "Antartic Arms" of Juan Miramontes y Suázola. The following códices are known: the one by Fray Valdez, already lost, reputed as the oldest (there is a copy of this codex made by Justiniani, preserved in the National Archives of Lima, Perú); the one of the Convent of Santo Domingo of Cuzco, which existed until 1900; the one of Sahuaraura, cited by Gonzales de la Rosa as from the Colony; the Harmsen or Paceño, seen by Tschudi in La Paz; Zegarra's, used by Gabino Pacheco for the French version.

The Peruvian Sebastian Barranca published the first Spanish version of the Ollantay in 1868. There are others: Fernando Nodal's (Vol. V—Elements of Quechuan grammar, 1874); Constantino Carrasco's, in verse (Lima, 1876); Bernardino Pacheco's, 1881; a Spanish translation of the French version by Gabino Pacheco (B. Universal, Madrid, 1883). In other languages there are the English translation by Clemente Marckham, and the German translations of Tschudi and Middendorf.

The action of the drama takes place in *Cuzco*. The era corresponds to the last days of the kingdom of *Pachacutec* and the first reigning years of his son *Tupac Yupanqui*. The principal sites of the action are the imperial palace, the fortress of *Ollantaytambo* and the *Ajllawuasi* (the House of the Selected). The development of the drama covers approximately 11 years. The dramatis personnae consist of: the two emperors already named, the generals Ollanta and Rumiñahui (Stone Eye), the chief Orco Waranca, Cusicoyllur (Star), Ima-Sumac (very beautiful) daughter of Ollanta and CusiCoyllur; the Villac-Uma (High Priest), Pikichaki (Swift footed) the merry one, confident and "third in command" of Ollanta; Pitu-Salla; Cusi-Coyllur's mother; virgins of the Sun, choruses, soldiers, and accompaniment.

The plot can be summarized as follows: Ollanta, the empire's most famous general, loves Cusi-Coyllur, Pachacutec's daughter, and she reciprocates his love. Marriage is impossible, according to Incan laws, because Ollanta is not of noble blood, even though he is Governor of the province of the Andes and wears, in honor of his exploits, the *champi* or golden helmet. The princess and the warrior maintain a secret relationship despite the invocations of the Villac-Uma, who is aware of the secret, and exhorts Ollanta to renounce his sacrilegious passion. Ollanta does not yield, and led by his passion, goes to the Inca to ask for his daughter in marriage. Pachautec tells him: "Remember that you are but a simple vassal; each one must remain in his place," and orders the seclusion of Cusi-Coyllur in the Ajllawuasi, where months later a daughter, Ima-Sumac, is born to the princess.

Having lost hope of seeing his beloved, and rebelling against the inexorable laws of the empire, Ollanta decides to revolt against the emperor and marches to Ollantaytambo. The Incan troops sent to subjugate him, under the command of Rumiñahui, are defeated by Orco Waranca, Ollanta's lieutenant. Rumiñahui then resorts to a trick. He presents himself before Ollanta as having been punished and ridiculed by the Inca immediately after his defeat, and begs the protection of the rebel chief. Ollanta, deeply touched, accedes to the petition of the famous Rumiñahui. Once inside the fortress, on a night previously agreed upon, Rumiñahui opens the doors to the

Incan forces, who defeat without struggle the unwarned defenders. Ollanta and the main leaders are arrested and taken to Cuzco.

But Pachacutec was no longer the emperor. He had been succeeded by Tupac Yupanqui. The prisoners are taken into his presence. Their death is certain according to the laws of the empire. With a magnanimity without precedence, Yupanqui forgives the rebels, restores honors and privileges on Ollanta, frees Cusi-Coyllur, his sister, upon entreaties of Ima-Sumac, and betroths her to Ollanta.

The drama has a development of its own characteristics: lack of supernatural elements, geographical fidelity, swift juxtaposition of scenes like the cinema; separation of the protagonists—Ollanta, Cusi-Coyllur, who never come together until the end of the play; a vigorous dialogue, agile, and balanced; an unexpected denouement which sets an example; original utilization of the song and the chorus as elements of reinforcement, variety and dramatic distension; the presence of the "jester" as a counterpoise in the sentimental equilibrium of the drama.

Such characteristics, apart from the purity of the quechua in which it was written, its direct concordance with geography and tradition, its correspondence with historical references, its typical poetic technique, strengthen the opinion of those who maintain the authenticity of Incan origin of the Ollantay in both theme and form. This thesis, (with Sebastian Barranca, Vicente Fidel Lopez, Horacio Urteaga, Luis Valcárcel, Pacheco Zegarra, Constantino Carrasco, Jesús Lara, Francisco Pi y Margall), refutes the authors who defend "the complete colonial origin" of the Ollantay (Ricardo Palma, Bartolomé Mitre, Menéndez Pelayo, Arturo Obitas, Vaca Guzman, etc.) and confuses the defenders of the transactionist thesis (Ricardo Rojas, Riva Aguero), who admit the Incan origin of the theme, but believe the scenification and elaboration of the drama to be Spanish.

The first thesis is the proper one, if we judge the question dispassionately. The ones who oppose it have very weak arguments like the one about the division of the Ollantay in acts and dialogues (Spanish style) and the finding of words alien to the quechua in the text. A thorough examination of the drama reveals to us the peculiar technique of the author in linking the scenes cinematographically, moving the action to various settings, with an art inconceivable in the Spanish theatre. The Ollantay has fifteen stage changes. If we wanted to represent it faithfully we would have to use the modern rotary proscenium. The division into scenes and acts—warped by the hands of the copyists and revisers of the codices—we consider conventional and artificial, but it does not suffice to bastardize the spirit of the action or the superb structure of the drama. Insofar as the Spanish words interpolated in the text are concerned, we must also put the blame on the copyists. The interpolated "ay" can be an arbitrary substitution of the Quechua words "jay", "ayau", "juy". Concerning the word "asno" (ass), Vicente Fidel Lopez suggested that the accusative "asnuta" should have been used instead of "llamata". Basing his conclusions on the fact that the rhyme is regular, Jesús Lara explains convincingly enough that substitution and reinstates to its proper place the substituted vocable:

—*Pikichaki*—Uj llamata wataskata (I saw a tethered llama).

—*Ollanta*—Qampuni karqanta chaycan (You must have been the one).

—*Pikichaki*—Chaycha wiñan Kay kunkayka (Por eso habrá crecido mi pescuezo) (On account of it my neck must have grown).

The same author points out in his book (Quechuan Poetry) the following poetical particularities of the Incan drama, which are in open opposition to the preceptive laws of Spanish drama and poetry: total absence of synalepha; relative tolerance in the measure of the verses, considering the tonic structure of the words; freedom in rhythm as much in the placement as in the number of consonants; freedom to use blank verse.

Finally, let us see two other arguments against the Incan origin of the drama: the intervention of the "jester" and of the "happy ending". First we should ask ourselves if the Spanish theater possessed the universal monopoly to create characters and invent situations. As it would be ridiculous to believe this, the belief that the Quechuan Pikichaki and the clemency of the Inca must have had Spanish inspiration is quite candid. Besides the fact that in the empire jugglers, jesters and buffoons were not unknown, the "jester" of the Ollantay, as called by the chroniclers, has the rank of one of the main characters, and does not play a secondary or decorative role as in the Spanish theater. Pikichaki appears, some times, like a double or like an echo of the thoughts of Ollanta, and, in a general way, applies the counterweight of gaiety throughout the drama. His action represents an element of equilibrium, moderating and soothing. The drama interprets, in this way, the realistic philosophy of the Amautas in conceiving human life as a logic and constant mutation of gladness and pain.

In talking about the denouement we must repeat the adjective *original* and add the one of *instructional*. Had it been a denouement in the Spanish style, it would have simply ended with the Inca's pardoning of the rebels. The Incan drama goes one step further, an unusual one for the Spanish theater: it rescues Cusi-Coyllur and puts her in Ollanta's arms, upon Ima Sumac's entreaties, and by the mercy of Tupac Yupanqui, the new Inca. The lovers' reunion at the end of the drama—the only one staged—is another typical characteristic of the Ollantay, and of its Incan origin, inasmuch as the Spanish theater would not have disregarded a constant exhibition of the idyll during the whole drama. There is more: counteracting the occidental technique, the denouement exalts the Incan's majesty, as noted by the Peruvian Alberto Tauro, as the Inca presents himself before the world

84

as the arbiter of life and death, apart from the fact that his action legalizes accomplished facts in consenting to the marriage of Ollanta to Cusi-Coyllur. As always, besides profiting from the aesthetic ends of the drama, what is of prime importance in its conception is a concrete pedagogical objective, of politico-social purview, in accordance with the traditional educational directives of the Incan theatre.

Fray Valdez never imagined, when copying the drama for the first time, the resounding fame it would acquire with time, nor the spirited polemics inspired upon discussion of its origin and its literary value. The Ollantay, on account of its vigorous personalities, its original and magnificent theme, the poetic beauty of its songs, the skillful and dynamic play of human passions, constitutes the most extraordinary and qualified example of the aboriginal theater in America. In fame, literary value and immortality, it can be compared only to the Popol-Vuh, considered the richest mythological legacy of the pre-Columbian american cultures. Pacheco Zegarra was not mistaken when, in 1878, he averred that the *Ollantay was worth a whole literature.*

In order to judge the high poetic quality, the exquisite expression of its sentiments, the admirable metaphoric ability of the great poet or group of poets which composed the famous drama, we furnish below the first and third urpis which appear in the text to be sung in chorus, even though the translation from the original language to English does not give us an exact version of their beauty and emotive intensity.

The first urpi is sung to warn Cusi-Coyllur of the dangers of her passion. The *tuya* is taken as a symbol, an innocent bird that can find death in the place where it is looking for food. With the name of the bird a refrain is formed, which is constantly repeated after each verse:

> —*Stop, don't eat now,*
> *Tuya, tuyita mine,*
> *In the estate of the ñusta,*
> *Tuya, tuyita mine.*
>
> —*Please do not try to consume,*
> *Tuya, tuyita mine,*
> *All of the tempting corn.*
> *Tuya, tuyita mine.*
>
> —*The grain is still white,*
> *Tuya, tuyita mine,*
> *And the cobs are too tender,*
> *Tuya, tuyita mine.*
>
> —*There's a slingshot for the greedy,*
> *Tuya, tuyita mine,*
> *There'll be a trap for you,*
> *Tuya, tuyita mine.*

—Take a look at the "pishqaqa"
Tuya, tuyita mine,
Hanging like he is,
Tuya, tuyita mine.

—The poor one was destroyed,
Tuya, tuyita mine,
For having picked up a grain,
Tuya, tuyita mine.

—That's the way that always find
Tuya, tuyita mine,
A bird that has become careless,
Tuya, tuyita mine.

The third urpi, composed in stanzas of four feet, alternates verses of ten and five syllables in the translation. It is sung when Ollanta, accompanied by Pikichaki, is getting ready to leave from Cuzco to rebel against the Inca. The urpi is an inspired praise of the beautiful Cusi-Coyllur.

—I don't know why I suddenly lost
My urpillay.

Do you know her? Try to see her,
Among these valleys.

Her face is the acme of seductions.
Her name is Star. No one equals her.
Her look is a fountain of light.
Suns and moons rivalling
Over her forehead,
Happily shine.

Soft and dark are the two tresses
Of the Urpillay;
Her eyebrows shine like the rainbow
Over her face.
Soft sunshine after the dawning
Glimmers in the glory
Of her enchanting pupils.

When she raises the veil of her lashes,
There awakes the nest of radiance
Of her glances.

There is more than one lover's chest
That has blossomed
Under the incomparable bewitchment
Of the Urpillay.

Like the "achancara" flowers
Over the snow,
Shines the enchantment of her cheeks,

86

Two rows of pearls are shining
When she smiles.
Her breasts are two cotton blossoms,
Graceful and smooth is her lovely neck,

At the mere contact of her hands
I vibrate all over with love.

(Free translation from Quechua by A. A. L.).

—*Tuyita.* Diminutive of tuya, native dove.

—*Pishqaqa.* Quail.

TEXTUAL NOTES

⁵⁰Luis A. Sánchez, *Historia de América,* Edit. Ercilla, Santiago, Chile, 1943.

⁵¹ Sánchez, ob. cit.

⁵² A. Henestrosa, revista *Universidad de México,* México, Abril, 1952.

⁵³ Victor Van Hagen, *Realm of Incas,* The New American Library, New York, 1957.

⁵⁴ Arturo Capdevila, *Los Incas,* Edit. Labor, Buenos Aires, 1937.

⁵⁵ Julio C. Tello, *Discovery of the Chavin Culture in Perú,* American Antiquity, Vol. 9, New York, 1943.

⁵⁶ Fragmento del texto que acompañó el traslado de varias piezas anexas a las *Informaciones de Toledo,* que imprimió Jimenez de la Espada, Madrid, 1900.

⁵⁷ *Carta del virey Toledo a S. M. el Rey de España,* desde Cuzco, Perú, 10 de Marzo de 1572.

⁵⁸ Montesinos, *Memorias Antiguas Historiales y Politicas del Perú,* Lima, 1950.

⁵⁹ Montesinos, ob. cit.

⁶⁰ Luis Baudin, *El Imperio Socialista de los Incas,* Edit. Zig Zag, Santiago, Chile, 1943.

⁶¹ Garcilaso de la Vega, *Comentarios Reales,* Emecé Edit., Buenos Aires, 1943.

⁶² Bernabé Cobo, *La Historia del Nuevo Mundo,* Sevilla, 1890.

⁶³ J. José Acosta *Historia Natural y Moral de las Indias,* Edit. Fondo de Cultura Económica, México, 1940.

⁶⁴ Cristobal de Molina, Guamán Poma de Ayala, Bernabé Cobo, Polo de Ondegardo, etc.

⁶⁵ Antonio de la Calancha, *Crónica Moralizadora de la Orden de San Agustin,* Barcelona, 1639.

⁶⁶ Raúl Porras Barrenechea, *Notas para una Biografía del Yaraví,* El Comercio, 28 de Julio, 1946, Lima, Perú.

⁶⁷ Torres Rubio, José de Rodrigues, *Vocabulario,* Lima, Siglo XVIII.

⁶⁸ Gonzáles, Holguin, Vocabulario, Lima, 1779.

⁶⁹ P. Martín de Morúa *Historia del Origen y Genealogía Real de los Reyes Incas del Perú,* Edit. Loayza, Lima, 1946.

⁷⁰ Bernabé Cobo, ob. cit.

—*Ajlla*. Chosen woman for the service of the Sun.

—*Ajlla-wasi*. Sacred house of the chosen women.

—*Achancaray*. Flower of the mountains.

—*Amauta*. Philosopher, historian, and poet.

—*Anacu*. Women underwear.

—*Anti*. People from the East.

—*Antisuyo*. Eastern region.

—*Apu*. Lord, chief, captain.

—*Ayllu*. Family—community—clan—race.

—*Awara*. Fable.

—*Chasqui*. State couriers.

—*Chumpi*. Belt, sash.

—*Churachikuy*. To subscribe.

—*Churanapata*. Shelf.

—*Hararec*. Meter of the Incan poetry, metrical art.

—*Harawi*. Name of a type of poetry.

—*Haravicus*. Poets. "Inventors" of Incan lyric poetry.

—*Huarachicoy*. Festivity of Huari.

—*Huari*. God of Manhood.

—*Illapa*. Lightning.

—*Inka*. Emperor.

—*Inti*. The Sun.

—*Inti-watana*. Sun dial.

—*Inti-Raymi*. The great festivity of the Sun.

—*Kausay-ttaqwiy*. History.

—*Kuntur*. Cóndor.

—*Kuntur-Cancha*. Kuntur's abode. Name given to Pachacutec's palace.

—*Korikancha*. The golden temple of the Sun.

—*Koya*. Empress.

—*Kosko*. Cuzco, capital of the Incan Empire, "The world's navel".

—*Llactaruna*. Native.

—*Llautu*. Scarlet insignia of supreme power.

—*Lliklla*. Women shawl.

—*Mamaqocha*. Sea.

—*Mamakuna*. Noble lady.

—*Mamapacha*. The earth-mother.

—*Maskaipacha*. Pompon of gold threads to hang down over the Inka's forehead.

—*Ñusta*. Princess.

—*Pakaritambo*. Place of the day-break.

—*Poquekancha*. Library.

—*Purumpacha*. Time in which nothing existed.

—*Pututo*. Trumpet (of sea shell).

—*Qelqay.* To write.

—*Quillqa.* Tablets, writing pads.

—*Quipus.* Lit. Knots. Statistical and accounting system used in the Incan empire. Made of knotted strings of different colors and thicknesses.

—*Quipucamayoc.* "Reader of quipus".

—*Runa.* Man, people.

—*Runaman-cchusty.* To civilize.

—*Runasimi.* Lit. General language of the men. Official language adopted by the nations confederated in the Incan Empire. The name Quechua was given by the linguist of the XVI century.

—*Simi.* Language.

—*Suyu.* Region.

—*Tampu.* State store-house-road relay.

—*Tahuantinsuyu.* The Incan Empire (the four parts of the world: Antisuyu, Collasuyu, Cuntisuyu and Chinchaysuyu).

—*Tampu-tuqo.* Mountain of the "four windows".

—*Taki.* Song. Also feast. (From the verb *takiy,* to sing).

—*Tinya.* Drum.

—*Tuya.* A bird.

—*Urpillay.* Dearest dove. (suf. of endearment).

—*Urpi.* Dove. Lyric poem.

—*Willaq-Uma.* The high priest.

—*Willakiy.* History.

—*Wiraqocha.* Supreme divinity.

—*Yachachisqa.* Disciple.

—*Yachachiy.* To teach, instruct.

—*Yachachiq.* Teacher, instructor.

—*Yachay.* To learn.

—*Yachaywasi.* School.

GENERAL BIBLIOGRAPHY

Acosta, José de, *Historia Natural y Moral de las Indias,* Edit. San Marti, Lima, 1922.

Alexander, Hartley Burr, *The Mythology of all Latin American Races,* Boston, 1930.

Anchorena, José Dionisio, *Gramatica Quecha,* Lima, 1847.

Arias-Larreta, Abraham, *Radiografia de la Literatura Peruana,* P. I. Amautas y Haravicus, Edit. Sayari, Trujillo, Perú.

————, Literaturas Aborigenes, 8th Edition, The New World Library, Los Angeles, Calif., 1963.

Arriaga, Pablo José de, *La Extirpación de la Idolatria en el Perú,* Edit. San Marti, Lima, 1920.

Baudin, Luis, *L'Empire Socialite des Inkas,* Institut d'Ethmologie, Paris, 1938, Edit. Zigzag, Santiago, Chile, 1943.

Barranca, José S., *Ollanta,* Lima, 196?.

Beltroy, Manuel, *Literatura Precolombina,* Rev. Letras, No. 21. Lima, 1924.

Bennet, Wendell, *Excavations at Tiahuanacu,* Anthropological Papers of the American Museum of Natural History, New York, 1934.

————, *Chimu Archaeology,* The Scientific Monthly, Vol. XLV, New York, July, 1937.

Betanzos, Juan Diez de, *Suma y Narración de los Incas,* Edit. San Marti, Lima, 1924.

Bingham, Hiran, *La Ciudad Perdida de los Incas,* Edit. Zigzag, Santiago, Chile, 1950.

Cabello de Balboa, Miguel, *Historia del Perú,* bajo la dominación de los Incas, Edit. San Marti, Lima, 1920.

Calancha, Fray Antonia, *Cronica Moralizada de la Orden de San Agustin en el Peru,* Barcelona, 1639.

Carrion Cachot, Rebeca, *La Cultura Chavin,* Revista del Museo Nacional, Vol. II, No. 1, 1948.

Cieza de Leon, Pedro, *Crónica del Perú,* Espasa-Calpe, Madrid, 1932.

Cobo, Bernabé, *Historia del Nuevo Mundo,* Sevilla, 1890.

Cossio, Felix, *Contribución al Estudio de la Prehistoria Peruana,* Cuzco, 1915.

Declaracion de los Quipucamayocs a Vaca de Castro. Library of Documents of Peruvian History, Vol. III, 2a. Ser. Edit. San Marti, Lima, 1920.

D'Harcourt, Raoul et Marie D. *Le Musique des Incas et ses Survivances,* Paris, 1926.

D'Harcourt, Margarite Bechard, *Melodies Indianes,* Equator-Perou-Bolivia, Milan, 1923.

Estete, Miguel de, *Relacion de la Conquista del Perú,* Edit. San Marti, Lima, 1924.

Farfan Ayerbe, J. M., *El Drama Quechua Apu-Ollantay,* Edit. Politec. José Pardo, Lima, 1952.

Fernandez, Diego, el Palentino, *Historia del Perú.* Primera Parte: Edit. Lucas de Torres, Madrid, 1913. Segunda Parte, Edit. Manuel de Odriozola, Vol. IX, Lima, 1876-77.

Fernández de Oviedo, Gonzalo, *Sumario de la Natural Historia de las Indias,* Madrid, 1855.

Garcilaso de la Vega, Inca, *Comentarios Reales,* Edit. Emece, Buenos Aires, 1943.

Herrera, Fortunato, *Filología Quechua Botánica Etnológica*. Revista del Museo Nacional, Tomo II, No. 1., Lima, 1948.

Horkeimer, Hans, *El Perú Prehispánico*, Edit. Cultura Antártica, Lima, 1950.

Hodlicka, Alex, *Early Men in South America*, Washington, 1912.

Jerez, Pedroisco de, *Verdadera Relación de la Conquista del Perú y Provincia del Cuzco*, Madrid, 1822.

Jimenez de la Espada, Marcos, *Relaciones Geográficas de Indias*, Madrid, 1881.

Krickberg, Walter, *Etnologia de América*, Mexico, 1946.

Lara, Jesús, *La Poesía Quechua*, Edit. F. C. E., Mexico, 1943.

Larco Hoyle, Rafael, *Los Mochicas*, Vol. I, Lima, 1938.

Lizárraga, Reginaldo, *Descripción de las Indias*, Edit. F. Loayza, Lima, 1946.

Lopez de Gómara, Francisco, *Historia General de las Indias*, Madrid, 1887.

Means, Phillip Ainsworth, *Ancient Civilization of the Andes*, New York, 1942.

Mitre, Bartolomé, *Ollantay*, Buenos Aires, 1881.

Middendorf, F. W., *Dramatische und Lyrische Dichtungen der Keshua, Sprache*, Leipzig, 1891.

Molina, Cristobal de, *Relación de las Fabulas y Ritos de los Incas*, Edit. F. Loayza, 1943.

Morúa, Fray Martin de, *Los Orígenes de los Incas*, Edit. F. Loayza, Lima, 194?.

Ondegardo, Polo de, *Información acerca de la Religion y Gobierno de los Incas*, Edit. San Marti, Lima, 1930.

Prescott, William, *History of the Conquest of Perú*, Edit. American Library, New York, 1956.

Poma de Ayala, Guaman, *Primera Nueva Corónica y Buen Gobierno*, Edit. Posnansky, La Paz, Bolivia, 1944.

Posnansky, Arthur, *Tiahuanacu, the Cradel of American Men*, New York, 1946.

Rojas, Ricardo, *Un Titan de los Andes* (Ollantay), Buenos Aires, 1939.

Rouma, Georges, *Le Civilization des Incas et leur Comunisme*, Brusels, 1924.

Santa Cruz, Pachacuti, Y., *Relación de Antiguedades de este Reyno del Perú*, Edit. San Marti, Lima, 1920.

Tello, Julio, *Las Primeras Edades del Perú*, Rev. Museo Nacional, Lima, 1939.

——————, *Orígen y Desarrollo de las Civilizaciones Pre-historicas Andinas*, Lima, 1942.

——————, *El Descubrimiento de la Cultura Chavin*, Lima, 1944.

——————, *La Expedición Arqueológica al Marañón*, Bol. Sociedad Geografica No. 55, 1938.

Urteaga, Horacio, *El Imperio de los Incas*, Edit. San Marti, Lima, 1931.

Tschudi, J. J., *Contribuciones a la Hisotria, Civilización y Linguistica del Peru Antiguo*, Edit. San Marti, Lima, 1918.

Uhle, Max, *Las Antiguas Culturas del Perú*, Bibl. San Marcos, Lima, 1918.

Valcárcel, Luis, *Del Ayllu al Imperio*, Edit. Garcilaso, Lima, 1925.

Valdizán, Hermilio, *Historia de la Medicina Peruana*, Lima, 1944.

Vidal, Leopoldo, *Literatura Inca*, Lima, 1947.

Villarán, Acisclo, *La Poesía en el Imperio de los Incas*, Lima, 1874.

Vienrich, Adolfo, *Azucenas Quechuas por unos Parias*, Tarma, 1905.

Wassen, Henry, *"The Ancient Peruvian Abacus"*, Goteburg, Vol. IX, 1931.

IV

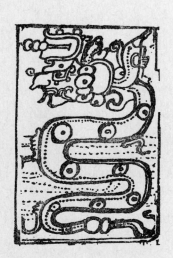

MAYA - QUICHE LITERATURE

(Quiché Language)

"Of all American peoples, the Quichés of Guatemala have left us the richest mythological legacy. Their description of the Creation, as given in the Popol Vuh, which may be called the national book of the Quichés, is in its rude strange eloquence and poetic originality, one of the rarest relics of aboriginal thought".[71]

"The Popol Vuh, or Sacred Book of the ancient Maya-Quiché, as it has been happily subtitled, is, beyond any shadow of doubt, the most distinguished example of native American literature that has survived the passing centuries."[72]

Neither Bancroft's nor Morley's words are exaggerated on judging the Popol Vuh. The splendid Maya-Quiché creation sometimes rivals and sometimes surpasses the philosophical depth and the imaginative power of the most famous theogonical legends of the world. And it is, at the same time, an epic of high literary quality and, possibly, the most brilliant expression of the ancient American mind.

The glory of the famous creation belongs to the Quiché people, Indians of Mayan ancestors, and inhabitants of the Guatemala highlands in the pre-Conquest era. As the most powerful nation of that time, the Quichés had to face the war of invasion at the arrival of the Spaniards, and they fought fiercely against Pedro de Alvarado sent by Cortez, in 1524. After their first defeats, the Quichés changed tactics and tried to attract Alvarado into the tortuous streets of Utatlan, the capital city, where the Spanish cavalry would be unable to operate. Alvarado, suspecting the stratagem, marched back to the open field in order to organize the attack of the infantry and assault the city. The Spanish troops seized Utatlán, massacre its population, and executed the king and most of the Indian nobles. Then, Utatlán was razed. To explain his behavior, Alvarado said in a letter written to Cortez ". . . and since I knew their unwilling disposition toward our Majesty . . . and for the sake of good and peace of this land . . . I ordered to burn the city and then raze it to the foundations . . . for it was so strong and dangerous that it seems more like a thieves' house than a peoples' dwellings . . ."[73]

Headed by some nobles and priests, the Indians survivors moved to the next town, Chichicastenango, named by the Spaniards Santo Tomás de Chichicastenango, where, years later, the missionaries of the Dominican order founded a monastery. A Father with the name of Francisco Ximenez was among the monks of that monastery, at the beginning of the eighteenth century. After mastering the Quiché language, and upon gaining the confidence of some important Indians, Father Ximenez was able to get the first information about "a secret and sacred book with the whole history of the Indians."

It seems that the precious narration of the mentioned book was first reduced to writing in the first years of the Conquest, by an unknown Indian, who have already learned Spanish. Father Ximenez transcribed the original Quiché text and translated it into Spanish, under the title of "Historia del orígen de los indios de esta Provincia de Guatemala" (History of the origin of the Indians of this province of Guatemala). This is the existing manuscript; the original is now lost. The Quiché narration is known as the Popol Vuh, Popol Buj, Council Book, Book of the Community, the Sacred Book, National Book of the Quichés, and History of the Quiché Nation.

Father Ximenez wrote that having no books to know the history of the Guatemalian, he decided to transcribe (verb and verbum) all their "tales", and translate them into Spanish language from the Quiché language, in which he found they had been written, from the time of the Conquest . . ." for it was then, that they changed their way of writing to ours; but it was with great reserve that these manuscripts were kept among them". Ximenez adds "On inquiring about this matter, while I was in the parish of Santo Tomas Chichicastenango, I found out that it was the doctrine they first imbided with their mother's milk, and that all of them knew it almost by heart, and I learned that they had many of these books among them."[74]

THE WRITING SYSTEM

Fray Bartolomé de las Casas, Bishop of Chiapas, and one of the missionaries better acquainted with life and traditions of the Indians, reported that the Indians of Guatemala and Mexico had chroniclers and historians, who knew everything about their religious rites and philosophy, the founding of cities, the history of kings and lords. "They have five books of figures and characters", he said, "and they made their large books with such craftsmanship, that can be said that our writings are not better than theirs. Some of the books were seen by our clergy, and even I saw part of those which were burnt by the monks, apparently because they thought that such books could harm the Indians' beliefs during the conversion."[75]

Father Alonso Ponce, who visited Yucatán in 1526, affirms that the Mayas of that region were praised for three things, the first of which was the knowledge and use of characters and letters to write their histories, ceremonies, calendars, rites and sacred sacrifices, "in books made of the bark of certain tree. These books are composed of long strips—a quarter or a third of Spanish *vara*—in width, and they were folded and evened in such a way that, when finished, they looked like the books bound in quarto".[76]

Several chroniclers, written in the first years of the Conquest, are full of references and testimonies on the existence of an aboriginal writing system. Among them we have that of Herrera Tordesillas, confirming the information about "the natives books which were found in Yucatán and Honduras," and that of López de Gómara, who says that "the Indians of Nicaragua have books of paper and parchment, more or less one hand in width by twelve hands in length, folded like bellows . . . and used on both sides to record in blue, purple, and other colors the historical events."[77]

Bernal Díaz del Castillo, author of the most fascinant history of the conquest of New Spain, refers that "the Mexican Indians had books made of the bark of a tree named a m a t e."[78] At the end of the seventeenth century some of these books were discovered in Guatemala (Petén), in the time the Spaniards made their expedition against the Itzá, 1696. Father Ximenez says that such books "were written with characters of close resemblance to those used by Hebrews and Chinese." Probably they were books written in Mayan hieroglyphics, and it is possible "that they even may be the same códices which were taken to Europe, and are now preserved in Dresden, Paris and Madrid."[79]

The oldest testimony about the aboriginal writing system, was given by the unknown Indian who wrote the Manuscript of Chichicastenango. He affirmed that the Quiché people had "a great book of pictures" with a description of the events and predictions of the future. This information was confirmed by Alonso Zorita, who said that "he had learned the political system of the Quichés through the pictures the Indians used to write their history, and from oral information given by the oldest Indians."[80]

THE SIXTEENTH CENTURY MANUSCRIPT

An unknown, but highly educated Quiché Indian, is supposed to be the author of the original manuscript of Chichicastenango, containing the Popol Vuh. This original redaction in Quiché language was reduced to writing, in Latin characters, at the middle of the sixteenth century. The anonymous author made reference to the existence of "an original book written long ago . . . but which sight is hidden to the searcher and the thinker." He decided "to bring it to light because now the Popol Vuh, as it is called, can not be seen any more."[81]

"The truth is," Father Ximenez comments, "that the mentioned book never has been seen . . . and we can not know if the Quiché writing was by painting, as those of México."[82]

It has not been determined yet the original source from which the Popol Vuh was taken. Genet and Chelbatz sustain the opinion that "the Popol Vuh is a translation of a manuscript written in hieroglyphs."[83]

Bancroft agrees with the existence of "a truly original book, which was destroyed or lost." The manuscript made in the sixteenth century would be "a literal copy, expressly made in order to replace the original Indian book, no longer available."[84]

Father Ximenez strongly believed in the perpetuation of the Quiché traditions by paintings. Schuller, a contemporary author, shares Ximenez' belief, adding that "the Popol Vuh possibly has been the interpretation not of one, but of many Quiché books of paintings."[85]

Authors Muller[86] and Spence,[87] without discussing the possible existence of some kind of Quiché written texts, believe that the Popol Vuh is a narration preserved by oral transmission, and finally reduced to writing, in Latin characters, by the unknown author of the Chichicastenango manuscript.

Abbe Brasseur de Bourbourg believes that the narration of the Popol Vuh" appears to have been written in part from memory, following ancient originals, and in part from the Sacred Book of the Quichés."[88]

Nobody, however, has advanced the slightest doubt on the Popol Vuh aboriginal authenticity, and, by an unanimous judgment, it is considered one of the most brilliant and representative fragments of the ancient American literature.

THE POPOL VUH — VERSIONS AND TRANSLATIONS

At the end of the seventeenth century Father Francisco Ximenez, then a parish priest of the village of Santo Tomas Chichicastenango, made the first transcription, and the first Spanish translation, of the Popol Vuh sixteenth century manuscript. A copy of this original and literal translation into Spanish, was published for the first time in Vienna, 1857, by Carlos Scherzer. It had been taken from the Ximenez' manuscript, in the library of the University of San Carlos, Guatemala.

A French americanist, Charles Ettiene Brasseur de Bourbourg, who arrived in Guatemala in 1855, was fortunate enough to gather one of the richest collections of old Guatemalan manuscripts. Listed in his collection was the priceless volume "Arte de las tres lenguas: Cakchiquel, Quiché, and Tzutuhil," written by Father Ximenez, at the end of which had been added the Ximenez' original translation of the Popol Vuh with the beginning "Este es el principio de las antiguas historias . . ." A volume, containing the Quiché text, and a French translation, was published by Brasseur de Bourbourg upon his returning to France, under the title "Le Livre Sacré et les Myths de l'antiquité Américaine, avec les livres héroiques des Quichés," (Paris, 1861).

When Brasseur de Bourbourg passed away, the volume of manuscripts, with the Popol Vuh, was bought by the American Edward E. Ayer, and incorporated to the linguistic collection, which was later donated to the Newberry Library of Chicago. Dr. Adrián Recinos visited this library in 1941, and found the volume listed just as "Arte

98

de las 'tres Lenguas," without mention to the Popol Vuh manuscript. After the pleasant surprise of finding the precious manuscript, Dr. Recinos made a careful comparison between the original text, written by Ximenez, and the French translation by Brasseur de Bourbourg, and on finding some differences, important omissions, and certain changes that affected the correct interpretation of the document, he decided to undertake a new version. The possibility of clarifying and correcting passages in the existing translations, stimulated his desire to intend this version directly from the original Quiché into Spanish. Thus, in his own words "by making use of the work of my predecessors in this field, I would somewhat advance knowledge of the document that Bancroft has called the most valuable heritage we have received from aboriginal American thought."[80]

Other Spanish versions of the Popol Vuh are those of Juan Gavarrete (Guatemala, 1872-73), which was reproduced by Santiago Barbarena (1905), and reprinted by Santiago Mimenza Castillo (1923); Antonio Villacorta and Flavio Rodas (Guatemala, 1927), J. N. Gonzalez and Angel Asturias (1923). Another French version was published by Georges Reynauld (Paris, 1925), and two more versions in German have appeared: one by Noa Elieses Pohorilles (Leipzig, 1913) and the other by Leonhard Schultze (Stuttgart, 1944). The most complete version in English is that of Adrián Recinos (Oklahoma, 1950).

Among the several, and highly recommendable works of interpretation devoted to the Popol Vuh, deserve special mention those of Walter Krichever, Edward Seller, Lewis Spence, Rudolph Schuller, Max Muller, Daniel Brington, Adrián Recinos, Rafael Girard and Angel Asturias.

LITERARY AND HISTORICAL VALUE

The Popol Vuh is "a great historical document," "a priceless legacy from the American mythic ages," " a delightful narrative poem, rich in adventures and imagination"; "it is a book of symbolical narrations, of dynastic sidereal myths, of theocratic rituals with roots in the night of the history, a book of great beauty and supreme wisdom."

They are words of different authors about the literary masterpiece created by the Quichés. The Popol Vuh, can be added, is that and much more. Its study and interpretation would demand many volumes. The Popol Vuh is a great conception, both mythological and historical. Its first part, dealing with the origin of the world and the creation of men, has a philosophical value in no way inferior to the theogonies and cosmogenesis of the occidental world. Its second part, devoted to narrate the deeds of Hunahpú and Ixbalanqué, has the vivacity, grace and wisdom of the most celebrated epic legends. A few narrations of the world literature posses the fascinating animation of the Popol Vuh. It is fresh, vivid and stimulating," as a book of short stories for children," said Father Ximenez, its discoverer. Attracted by its powerful originality some modern authors have used the Quiché book as source of inspiration (the German Krikerberg, the English Charles Finger: "Tales from Silver Lands," New York, 1924), and a great epic poem has been written in Germany to relate the adventures of Hunahpú and Ixbalanqué, the young American Demigods (Oswald Claassen, Die Abuen des Mondes, Das Gefass des Schicksals, Krefeld, Germany, 1933).

In the Popol Vuh we find the magic participation of the animals, as in the Ramayana; the alternation of daring adventures in quimerical regions, and pleasant common episodes of everyday life, as in the Odyssey and, as in the Iliad, we contemplate the intervention of the Gods in the human struggle. Besides its outstanding imaginative qualities, the book has a placid sense of humor, and emphasizes a very singular attitude of the man on facing his fate in the world.

Rafael Girard,[90] a noted scholar and interpreter of the Maya-Quiché culture, has affirmed that the Popol Vuh has not two independent parts, one historical and one mythical. In his opinion the mythical narrations are historical narrations, as well, and that they form a solid and coherent body of narrations to which the name of Maya-Quiché Mytho-history would be more properly given.

The same author has made the observation that the manuscript of the Popol Vuh is not divided into chapters, that it has continuity from beginning to end, thus revealing a singular modality of the Maya-Quiché mind. This modality is also maintained in the chronological system of the Maya-Quichés. All the calendaric series are linked, without interruptions, following the example of the Cosmic order. The chrono-magical system, then, is patterned upon the Cosmic models, and these models are, in fact, the archtypes for any elaboration of the Maya-Quiché mind. In no other way the Maya-Quichés could have been able to live and perpetuate an unbroken continuity of the past. The past has no dark zones for them. In this living perpetuation of the past, we can find the basic roots of their cultural consciousness.

Originally and basically the Maya-Quiché culture is, in effect, a mythological culture. A real knowledge of such culture would require a profound exploration of the indigenous mind, a scientific study of the Mytho-history with the help of the anthropological sciences. Above all, the study of the Maya-Quiché culture can have the invaluable help of the present ritual practices of the Indians, who still have and obey the same mythical archtypes that have been guiding the Maya-Quiché behavior for thousands of years.

Many authors concurred in the opinion that the Popol Vuh is the best example of the aboriginal sacred texts, and, possibly the most complete historical document of a native civilization. The narration starts in the remote ages of American pre-history, with the initial steps of man in our continent. It is then, the oldest testimony of human history in the world (the Rig Veda and the Zenda Avesta came later). In its first part, the creation of the world is narrated; the second part deals with the evolution of the Maya-Quiché culture from its origin up to its division into four ages or great cycles, three of which correspond to the pre-historical horizon, and one to the historical age.

The Popol Vuh is considered a complete encyclopedia of theogony, cosmogony and astrology. It contains genesis and development of gods, men, species and things. It has an explanation of the world creation, of the distribution of human beings and animals, of the relationship between men and gods, and of the ethical behavior of men in community, the proper organization of human societies, the aborigen life and its physical environment, the history and its concatenation of events. In short, it is the book of the Maya-Quiché culture and its development.

From the historiographical point of view, the techniques and philosophy of the book are surprisingly modern. History for the Maya-Quichés is not just a chronological inventory of events, official or not, but the dynamic and creative biography of the man and its community, within their own historical time and space.

Finally, let us remember that, in addition to the literary, historical and philosophical values, the splendid narration of the Popol Vuh has been corroborated by scientific testimonies from arqueology, linguistics, climatology, orography, geo-botany, anthropogeography, and the astro-theo-mathematical system Maya-Quiché.

In the next chapter a free and original version of some parts of the Popol Vuh are presented (Creation of the world—Creation of man). The complete text in English version will be published, together with the Incan drama Apu Ollantay, and an anthology of the Aztec poetry, in the book, already announced, under the title of "Pre-Columbian Literary Masterpieces."

TEXTUAL NOTES

[71] Hubert Howe Bancroft, *The Native Races of the Pacific States*, Vol., III, pag. 42, San Francisco.

[72] Sylvanus G. Morley, *Foreword*, in The Popol Vuh by Adrián Recinos, University of Oklahoma Press, 1950.

[73] Carta-relación de Pedro Alvarado a Hernán Cortez from Utatlán April 12, 1524. *Historiadores Primitivos de Indias*, Vol., XXII, XXVI. Biblioteca de Autores Españoles, Madrid, 1852-53, XXII, 458.

[74] Fr. Francisco Ximenes, *Historia de las Provincias de San Vicente de Chiapa y Guatemala*, Vol., i, 5, Sociedad de Geografia e Historia de Guatemala, Guatemala, 1929-31.

[75] Fr. Bartolomé de Las Casas, *Apologética Historia de las Indias*. Vol., I of "Nueva Biblioteca de Autores Españoles, Historiadores de Indias. Chap. CCXXXV.

[76] Fr. Alonso Ponce, *Relación Breve y Verdadera* de las Muchas Cosas que le Sucedieron al Padre Fray Alonso Ponce, en las Provincias de la Nueva España. Vol., LVII-LVIII. Colección de Documentos para la Historia de España, Madrid, 1873. II, 392.

[77] Lopez de Gómara, *Historia General de las Indias*. Historiadores Primitivos de Indias. Vol. XVII-XXVI, Biblioteca de Autores Españoles, Madrid. XXII, 284.

[78] Bernal Diaz del Castillo, *Verdadera Historia de la Conquista de la Nueva España*, Mexico, 1941.

[79] Adrián Recinos, *The Popol Vuh*, 1946, p. 20.

[80] Alonso Zorita, *Breve y Sumaria Relación de los Señores de la Nueva Espana*, Mexico, 1892, pp. 225-26.

[81] Francisco Ximenez, Preamble. *The Popol Vuh*, manuscript, XVI cent.

[82] ————, *La Historia de los Indios de esta Provincia de Guatemala*, Edit. C. Scherzer, Vienna, 1857, p. 101.

[83] Genet et Chelbatz, *Histoire des Peuples Maya-Quiches*, Paris, 1927.

[84] Hubert Howe Bancroft, *The Native Races*, Vol. II, p. 42.

[85] Rudolf Schuller, *Der Verfasser des Popol Vuh*. Anthropos. Vol., XXVI, 5-6, Sept.-Dec., 1931.

[86] F. M. Muller, *Chips from a German Workshop*, London, Vol., I, p. 309-37.

[87] Lewis Spence, *The Popol Vuh*: The Mythic and Heroic Sagas of the Kiches of Central América, Chicago, 1908, 31.

[88] Abbe Brasseur de Bourbourg, *Histoire des Nations Civilisees du Mexique et l'Amerique Centrale*, Paris, 1857, Vol., LXXX.

[89] Adrián Recinos, *The Popol Vuh*, México, 1946, Prolog., p. 10.

[90] Rafael Girard, El Popol Vuh, Fuente Histórica, Guatemala, 1952.

V

THE
POPOL VUH

PREAMBLE

This is the beginning of the old traditions here, in the Quiché. We are going to write the old stories, the beginning and origin of everything that was done in the Quiché nation, the nation of the Quiché Indians. And here we shall reveal all that was hidden, the great revelations by Tzacol, and Bitol (the Maker, the Creator), Alom and Qaholom (God-mother and God-father) as they are called, Hunahpú-Vuch, Hunahpú-Utiú, Zaquí-Nimá-Tzíis, Nim-Ac, Tepeu, Gucumatz, u Qux Cho, u Qux Paló, Ah Raxá Lac, and Ah Raxá Tzel.[1] And we shall tell what the Quiché chronicles said about Xpiyacoc and Xmucané, helpers and protectors,[2] and we shall tell what they did at the time the light and the first words came out in the world.

We are writing under the law of the Christian God, and we have decided to fix and perpetuate our narration because the Popol Vuh, the original book, is no longer available. Great were the descriptions and the account of the old book of how the sky and earth were formed, of how all was divided into fourth parts, and of how the universe was measured, and its four angles determined and fixed,[3] as directed by the Maker and the Creator, the Mother and the Father of life, of all created things, the Mind of Heaven, the divine mind that watches over the happiness of the people, and is permanently present in the goodness given to man, and to all what exists on the sky, on the earth, and on the sea.

---

[1] These are the names of the divinities, in pairs or couples as it is used by the Quichés.

—*Tzacol and Bitol,* Creator and Maker.

—*Alom,* the Mother-God.
Qaholom, the Father-God.

—*Hunahpú-Vuch,* God of the Dawn. (feminine)
Hunahpú-Utiú, God of the Night. (masculine)

—*Zaquí-Nimá-Tzíis,* mother of God, and her consort *Nim-Ac.*
—*Tepeu,* king or sovereign.

Gucumatz (guc: green feathers—cumatz: serpent). Serpent of green feathers. It is the Quiché version of Kukulcán, Maya name for Quetzalcoatl.

—*U Qux Cho,* god or spirit of the lake.
U Qux Paló, god or spirit of the sea.

—*Ah Raxá Lac,* Lord of the Earth. (the green plate)
A Raxá Tzel, Lord of the Sky. (the blue bowl)

2 *Xpiyacoc* (the Grandmother) and *Xmucané.* "This is the active creator couple, who are directly concerned with the making of material things" (Palacios).

3 "To found the dimensions, and fix the limits of the Cosmos," was the first task in the creation of Universe. The Cosmos was divided into four quadrangular juxtaposed planes, and named sky and earth. Then, the angles, lines, distances and basic points were fixed at once and forever. The Creators established in this way the geometric, astronomic, and ritual patterns to be followed from then on. Maya-Quiché priests and peasants have continued in the use of the same divine rules to quadrangle farms, millpas, plazas, and patios of altars and temples. In a milenary repetition of the cosmic model, the same pattern has been imitated in cosmogony, theogony, calendars, rites, mathematics, chronology, astronomy, family, society, and government.

But the cosmic quadrangle, as observed by Girard, has no correspondence with the four cardinal points; the correspondence is with the solstices. The quadrangle is divided into four parts by the astronomic cross, which is oriented toward the cardinal routes.

The four main gods, cited in the Popol Vuh, have a symbolical position in the giant quadrilateral limited by the solstices, and formed by Sun and Moon during their motions of rotation and translation. Each cosmic angle, where the celestial body stops, is marked as a limit of the world—like the *ahcantun* of the Maya tradition—and each of the extreme positions of the sun is considered as a theogonic entity with particular name, character, and functions, but only as a divine part of the supreme deity situated in the zenith.

FIRST PART

1

This is the first narration, the first narration of the Beginning, when everything was in calm, still, silent.

It was the Beginning: there were neither trees nor stones. There was no grass, no animal, no human being. There were neither birds nor mountains; neither wind nor light.

The earth had not emerged yet. There were only the waters, in calm, and the empty sky.

There was nothing as a whole. Nothing with motion or sound. Nothing was standing. Nothing existed.[1]

It was the Beginning. Everything was motionless, in suspense, into the night. Only the Creator, the Founder, Tepeu, Gucumatz, the Progenitors were there in the darkness, over the waters, surrounded by light.[2] They were under green and blue feathers, possessed by great feelings, by high thoughts. In this manner existed the Mind of Heaven, Huracán.[3]

It was in the darkness that Tepeu and Gucumatz came together, and started talking. And the first words came out to life. They talked, exchanging feelings and thoughts, discussing and deliberating, and finally agreed, upon meditation, about the birth of life, and the creation of world. It was thought and decided there, in the night, under the inspiration of Huracán, Mind of Heaven.

"So may it be! Thus let it be done, as we have thought!," they said, "Be the emptiness filled! That the earth emerge and be affirmed! Let the waters move and divide! That the dawn comes over all."

"Earth!", they said, and covered by fog, coming from a giant cloud of dust the earth appeared. Instantly the mountains grew up, valleys and coasts were formed, the trees emerged at once in forests of cypresses and pines.[4]

Then the currents of water were divided and the rivulers started running freely between the hills.

"Dawn!", they said afterwards, and the dawn appeared over the world.

"How great was your inspiration oh! Huracán, Mind of Heaven," Gucumatz joyfully exclaimed.

"Our task shall be finished," was the answer.

Thus was the first work of the Creation, inspired by Mind of Heaven, and Mind of Earth.[5] It was made by a prodigy, when nothing existed, empty was the sky, unknown the earth. When everything was in suspense, motionless, into the night of the Beginning.

2

"And now, will be there only silence and quietness under the trees, within the forest, under the shrubs and bushes, along the ravines?", said the Progenitors, "It can not be so!"

And came the creation of the animals, the small and wild animals, to be guardians of the woodlands, inhabitants of the thickets and gorges, named deer, puma, jaguar, birds, snakes.

"You deer, you puma, you jaguar, all of you will live in the forest, and in the gorges," these animals were told. "You will walk on four feet, live there, and be fruitful."

"You birds, to live on the trees and on the bushes. There you will stay, and get your food, and multiply."

When these and all animals were formed, the Creator, the Maker, the Progenitors told them: "Now speak to us. Do not be silent. Speak out our names, make an invocation to us, your Father, your Mother, Tepeu, Gucumatz, your Progenitors."

But the animals could not speak. They only screech, roar, warble, cackle, whim, hiss, and croak, each one according to its kind, each in a different way.

"It is not what we want," the Progenitors thought, "These beings can not speak out our names, they can not invoke and worship us." And they decided to try again.

"You are going to be changed"—the Progenitors said.

"You are unable to speak, and to recognize your creators. Keep your dwellings, but your body will be sacrificed, and it will be eaten. That is our decision. Accept your fate!"[6]

And the Progenitors tried to create new and better beings. This time they use mud to make them. But the work was not good at all. The body of the new beings was soft, had not firmness, it melted away. The new beings could talk this time, but they had not understanding, they could not move themselves, their sight was blurred, they had a stiffed head, a very long neck, and were unable to feel. The mud beings were destroyed.[7]

3

"How can we make the kind of being we want? . . . A being able to speak to us, a being with understanding, able to invoke and worship us?", said the Creator, the Maker, the Progenitors.

This time they decided to consult Ixpicané and Ixmucané, to Hunahpú-Vuch and Hunahpú-Utiú, the grand-mothers of the dawn, the grand-fathers of the dawn.

"Let's try again," they spoke to them "Set the date for the creation of new beings. Tell us how they shall be made, how they shall be fed, what they shall be made of, how we shall call them. And cast the lot again with your grains of corn and tzité, to know if we shall carve their mouth and eyes out of wood."

"Good luck, creatures!", said the Grand-mothers of the dawn, the Grand-fathers of the dawn," "Get together, and speak to us, you corn, you tzité! Tell us if the wood is the material to be carved for the new beings by the Creator, the Maker, the Progenitors."

Then they revealed the adivination: "The new beings made of wood will be able to exist, to walk, to speak, to multiply."

"So it may be," said the Progenitors, the Creator, the Maker. "We shall make beings of wood."

They started working in their creation, and it was finished very soon. The beings of wood looked more perfect, and they could speak. From the hands of the creators they scattered in all directions to populate the earth.

But they had neither soul nor mind. They did not know who they were, where they had come from, whom they were made by. They could remember nothing, they wandered aimless, and have to walk on all fours for their feet and legs had not strength. They spoke at first, but their faces were expressionless; they had neither blood nor flesh; their body was dry, they had no intestines, their head was empty, and they looked like automats.

So were these wooden figures. They no longer remembered their Progenitors, the Maker, the Creator, and Mind of Heaven. They were wooden beings without substance, blood, moisture, understanding, and senses.

4

It was just a trial, an unsuccessful trial. The men made of wood were not good, neither was the woman made of rushes. They did not understand, did not think, and did not remember. By decision of their creators the wooden figures were punished, broken up, anihilated, destroyed.

The punishment started with a heavy rain. The earth was darkened, and by day and by night a black rain fell down. Then appeared the so-called X e c o t c o v a c h to devour the eyes of the wooden figures; came C a m a l o t z, the cutter of heads; came out C o t z b a l a m to eat their flesh, and finally showed up T o c u m b a l a m to crumble, to torturate, to grind them.

All the animals came against them. The stones and sticks began to strike their faces, and the jars, plates, pots, griddles, and grinding stones they had used, fiercely revolted against the old masters.

"You have tormented us by day and by night, all the time. Now we shall grind your body," shouted the grinding stones.

"We were tortured in the fire by you. Look at our faces blackened with soot. Now you are going to know the fire. We shall burn you," spoke griddles and pots.

"We have suffered very much. You used to kill and eat us," said the birds, "Now we shall kill you."

"We were always hungry, and always looking at you. And you always have a stick ready to strike us, while you eat happily. Now you are going to know our teeth, because we shall devour your bodies," said the dogs.

The jars of boiling water also insulted them, and the hearth-stones hurled themselves straight from the fire to hit their heads.

The wooden figures could resist no longer the universal revolt against them. They started running as fast as they could. They ran in line, like grains of corn, one behind the other. They tried to climb the trees, and the trees bent to get rid of them. They tried to reach the roof of the houses, and the houses fell down to throw them away. They intended to gain refuge in the caves, and the caves repelled them at once. The wooden figures, full of panic, continued running in all directions, and collided, fell down into precipices, and they mangled finally one another.

So was the annihilation, the ruin, the end of the wooden beings.

By the old sayings we learned that there were some survivors, and that their descendants are the monkeys, animals that used to live in the forests, and have some human resemblance. And that they were permitted to remain, only to remind us that, once upon a time, wooden figures were populating the earth.[8]

THIRD PART

1

"The time of dawn is here. We must finish our work. Let man appear on the face of the earth," said the Progenitors, the Creator, the Maker, Tepeu, Gucumatz.

It was just before the sun, the moon and the stars had appeared. And the Creators, the Makers decided to form the man, the real men, the noble sons, the civilized vassals,

110

able to remember, to understand, to recognize, nourish and worship their Progenitors.

They came together, deliberated, and finally agreed in what they were going to do. The corn was selected this time as the material that should be used. It was the corn, the yellow and red corn discovered in P a x i l and C a y a l á by the animals H o h, Y a c, Q u e l, and U t i ú.

From the beautiful and rich lands of Paxil any Cayalá came the yellow and white ears of corn. There was abundant and delicious food of every kind in those lands—pataxte, zapotes, anonas, jocotes, natzas, and honey.

The yellow and white corn from Paxil and Cayalá was selected to form the man. Of corn was made the flesh of the first men. And the muscles, the vigor, the strength was given to them with the food of nine drinks, made of ground corn, by X m u c a n é.

2

B a l a m - Q u i t z é, B a l a m   A c a b, M a h y - c u t a h, and I q u i - B a l a m   were the names of the first men created. They had no father nor mother. They were not born of woman. They were created by miracle, by means of incantation by the Progenitors, the Creator, the Maker, Tepeu and Gucumatz. Because they had the appearance of men, they were men, and were called men.

As men, they were able to see, to hear, to walk, and to talk. They were strong, handsome and beings of good nature. They had intelligence and wisdom, and their sight and their knowledge could reach everything and everywhere in the world.

"What do you think of yourselves? Are you happy with your condition?", asked the Progenitores, the Creator, the Maker, Tepeu and Gucumatz.

"We really thank you our Creators," the first four men answered, "We speak, we hear, we walk, and we think. We can see and know everything near and far. We recognize you, we remember you, we are able to feel gratitude for you. Thanks, oh, Creators for our life, thanks for having created us, for having given us being."

The Progenitors, the Creators, however, were not satisfied with the answer. They thought that the new beings had received too much from them. They were supposed to be simple creatures not Gods, who could see all and take knowledge of all.

"Let's limit their power," they said.

And Mind of Heaven blew mist in the eyes of the four men, and their eyes clouded as when a mirror is breathed upon. From then on the human beings have been able to see and know only what is near them.[9]

Then, their wives were made. Mind of Heaven, God himself made them carefully. And they were sent, during the sleep, to lie down at the side of each man. The first four men felt their hearts filled with joy and happiness, when they awoke and found the four beautiful new beings lying down beside them. The names of the first women were C a h á - P a l u n a, C h o m i h á, T z u n u i h á, and C a q u i x a h á, and they became wives of Balam-Quitzé, Balam Acab, Mahucutah, and Iqui-Balam, in this order.

These four couples were our first fathers, our first mothers. They were the origin of us, of all of us, in the small and large tribes, past and present generations of the Quiché people.

1 There was something that existed before everything, the first Creator, only alluded in the Popol Vuh. It is possible that in the "old narrations," from which the Popol Vuh was taken, the references about the Supreme God have had resemblance with the beautiful version given by the Mayas in the *Chilam Balam de Chumayel:* "Everything was created by our Father God and through his word. Where neither sky nor earth did exist, there was already his Divinity, who became a cloud, and created the universe."

2 The light, surrounding them, expresses that they are Sun Gods, but they are not just material parts of the cosmos, but spiritual beings who insuflate life and divinity into the astral bodies. In other words, the Suns are not gods by themselves, but tangible expression of what they have of intangible nature. There is one sun, though its positions are different—and only one god polimorphically represented by the daily position of the sun.

3 The Maya-Quiché septemvirate of gods is complete with the mention of Mind of Heaven, Huracán, who is present when the other gods meditate, think, and reach trascendental decisions.

4 "Divine word" implies immediate creation. It is synonym of power and action. The gods met in the divine council, and after deliberation, they reached an unanimous decision. Having pronounced the exact word for e a r t h, the earth appeared.

5 "Mind of Earth," a new expression for "Mind of Heaven," who now is a God of Earth too. Huracán literally means "being of one foot." The mythological absence of Huracan's foot, reveals a theogonical concept by which it is asserted that a god is a divine part separated from the body of another god. Huracan, Mind of Heaven, without the foot of which the Earth was made is represented by the Mayan artists either by a bicephalous god or by the Sun-disc over the abdomen of the Earth goddess.

6 The Maya-Quiché code narrates the creation in four steps: first the sky, then the earth, and all what exists on the earth, following the accepted scientific order: minerals, vegetables, animals, and as a culmination, the human beings. After the creation of the world, the narration follows the development of life and culture, through the Maya-Quiché history.

In the *First Age* the early beings were created. They were unable to talk, recognize, and remember their Creators, however, and were transformed in animals, and condemned to live in caves, thickets, and gorges. It is a clear reference to the life of the primitive men. The punished beings could be killed and their body eaten, according to the divine law, by which it is established the practice of sacrifices (of animals, not human beings). The fact that the first beings intended to express their adoration to the Gods, and they could not understand each other, and could not talk in the same way because of this different language, it just the revelation of the linguistic heterogeneity of that remote age.

Destruction or transformation of the imperfect beings will be repeated once and again, until the Creators accomplish the creation of the perfect man, or archtype of the Maya-Quiché culture.

7 In the Second Age (or creation) the beings made of mud (as in the biblical genesis) represented an advance in the creation. The new beings could talk, but they had no understanding. And they were destroyed. This second ethnic cycle corresponds to the advance from the primitive economic system to the so-called period of the horticulture and invention of the pottery. At the same time the first American institutions appeared—economy, rites, communal system, etc.

The material used to form the "creatures" typifies the main characteristic of the cultural cycles: mud in the second period, wood in the third, and corn in the fourth.

8 The Council of Gods had a new meeting and decided that the four cosmic gods set the date for the new creation. In accordance with the mythical pattern of the first creation, the four gods must repeat the act of illuminating the world with the dawn. The gods are now Xpiyacoc and Xmucané, Hunahpú-Vuch and Hunahpú-Utiú, grandmothers of the dawn and grandfathers of the dawn.

The tzité is a product of the "palo de pito" (erythrina corallodendron L.) its form similar to the bean, and has a red color. Even now, as the gods in the third age, the Quiché priests make use of corn and tzité grains in their ritual adivinations.

Bean and corn form a divine couple in the Chortí theogony (corn: masculine rol- tzité: feminine rol). This sexual relationship helps to understand the representative role of each one in the history. Corn is the theogonic exponent of the fourth age, and its agrarian and patriarcal cycle; and tzité represents the third age, or the matrilineal-horticultural cycle.

The wooden figures of the third age could talk and procreate, but they did not feel. It seems that, in spite of the advances reached in the matrilineal horizon, the ethical ideals and the ideal wisdom of the Maya-Quiché archtype have not been conquered yet. The Gods decided to destroy the wooden figures "by death." The first appearance of the word death at this time, possibly correspond to the initiation of some complicated funeral rites.

The narration of the first creation ends with a reference to the "survivors," who had resemblance with the monkeys. The Popol Vuh place the relationship between man and monkey in opposite sequence to that of Darwin and Haeckel.

9 This period corresponds to the creation of the representative man of the Maya-Quiché culture. The fourth creation is made "before the sun, the moon and the stars had appeared," because the gods only work in the night. This time, it is said, the divine spirit entered in the birth of life. Being conscious of this divinity, the "men of corn" were able to pay spiritual tribute to their creators. God's advent into flesh and soul only occurred when corn was used to make the new beings; and the advent of the Maya-Quiché culture only occurred when

114

the corn became the food of man. The fourth creation means creation of human types representatives of the Maya-Quiché culture, and not just the origin of the human species. Similarly, the finding of corn in Paxil and Cayalá reveals the economic, social, and religious importance of corn at that time, and not the discovery of the plant, since the corn had been cultivated during prehistorical periods.

The men of the fourth creation were perfect. "They are our own sons," the Gods had said. The new beings spoke the language of the gods (what tells us that the linguistic unity has been reached by the Maya-Quichés). Because of their intelligence and other divine qualities, they were as perfect as God. The Maker, the Creator, the Progenitors did not consider convenient this equal status between men and gods. They gathered in the Divine Council, and by their decision Mind of Heaven blew mist into the eyes of the new beings, to limit their sight and knowledge.

The allegory is clear. The creators considered unwise to leave the men in that state of perfection. Men, by themselves, through wisdom and virtue should open their way toward the repossession of their divine omniciency and omnividency. Finally they shall recover the lost perfection.

GLOSSARY OF MAYA-QUICHÉ WORDS

—*Popol Vuh.* In literal translation "Book of the Community." *Popol,* Maya word, means "together" or "common house" *Popol na* means "house of the community where they assemble to discuss affairs of the republic," according to the Diccionary de Motuk. Father Ximenez says that "pop" is a Quiché verb and means " to gather" "to meet," and that "popol" means something that belongs to the municipal council, or "communal," "national" business. Popol Vuh, for Ximenez, means "Book of the Community" or "Book of the Council" or "National Book."—*Vuh,* from the Maya "huun" or "uun," has three related meanings: paper, book and tree (the bark of which was used to make the paper).

—*Gucumatz.* Liter. "Feathered serpent that lives in the water," (Bishop Núñez de Vega).

—*Huracán.* Liter. "Of one leg" "flush of a leg": Cuculhá-Huracán.

—*Nim Ac.* Liter. Great wild pig. Consort of Nimá-Tzíis.

—*Nimá-Tzíis.* Great white coati mundi (naqua nasica). Mother of god.

—*Tzité.* Eryhrina corallodendron.

—*Xpiyacoc.* Liter. Old woman (grandmother).

—*Xmucané.* (Consort of Xpiyacoc-Grandfather).

—*Hunahpú.* Liter. "Hunter with a blowgun." Ahpú, in Maya, means "hunter" also.

—*Xecotcovach.* "A bird, probably an eagle or a sparrow hawk," (Ximenez).

—*Camalotz.* Vampire (nima chicop).

—*Cotzbalam.* Jaguar.

—*Tucumbalam.* Danta or tapir (Recinos). Shark or crocodilae, (Seler).

—*Paxil.* "Spreading of the water."

—*Cayalá.* From "cay," rotten. Putrid matter in the water (Recinos).

—*Zapote.* Mamey, lucuma mammosa.

—*Cacao.* Cacau (Maya and Quiché).

—*Pataxte.* A variety of cacao (Thebroma bicolor).

—*Jocote.* Spondias purpurea.

—*Anona.* Quiché *cavex.* Chirimoya.

—*Nantze.* Byrsonyma crassifolia.

—*Yac.* Mountain cat.

—*Utiu.* Coyote.

—*Quel.* Small parrot.

—*Hoh.* Crow.

—*Balam-Quitzé.* "Jaguar of sweet laughter."

—*Balam-Acah.* "Jaguar of the night."

—*Mahucutah.* "Not brushed."

—*Iqui-Balam.* "Jaguar of Moon."

—*Cahá-Paluna.* Standing water.

—*Chomihá.* Beautiful, chosen water.

—*Tzununihá.* Water of hummingbirds.

—*Caquixahá.* Water of the Macaw.

BIBLIOGRAPHY

Alexander, Hartley Burr, *Mythology of All Races*. Vol., XI, Latin American Chap., V. Central America. Boston, 1920.

Bancroft, Hubert Howe, *The Native Races of the Pacific States,* San Francisco, 1883.

————, *History of Central America,* San Francisco, 1890.

Barela, Fr. Francisco, *Vocabulario Kakchiquel, Manuscript.* National Museum of Mexico.

Brasseur de Bourbourg, *Cartas para servir de introdución* a la historia primitiva de las naciones civilizadas de la América septentrional, México, 1851.

————, *Grammaire de la langue Quichee,* Paris, 1862.

Brinton, Daniel G., *The Maya Chronicles,* Philadelphia, 1882.

————, *The Annals of the Cakchiquels,* Philadelphia, 1885.

————, *The Native Calendar of Central America and Mexico,* Philadelphia, 1893.

Capdevila, Arturo, *El Popol Vuh para todos,* Guatemala, 1938.

Chilam Balam de Chumayel, English translation by Ralph L. Roys, Carnegie Institution. No. 483, Washington, D.C., 1933.

Claasen, Oswald, *Die ahnen des Mondes. Eine Indianische Edda,* Krefeld, 1933.

Finger, Charles J., *Tales from Silver Lands,* Garden City, New York, 1924.

Genet, Jean, *Revue des Études Maya-Quichées,* Vol., I, Paris, 1934.

Genet and Chelbatz, *Historie des peuples maya-quichés,* Paris, 1927.

Girard, Rafael, *El Calendario Maya-Quiché,* Mexico, D.F., 1948.

————, *Esoterismo del Popol Vuh,* Mexico, D.F., 1948.

————, *Historia del Origen y Desarrollo de los Civilizaciones Indoamericanas,* Guatemala, 1951.

————, *El Popol-Vuh, Fuente Histórica.* Vol., I, Guatemala, 1952.

Imbelloni, José, *El Génesis de los Pueblos Proto-históricos de América* Academia Argentina de Letras, Vol., VIII, No. 32, Buenos Aires, 1940.

————, *¿Qué significa Popol Vuh?* Actes du XXVIIIe. Congres International des Americanistes, Paris, 1948.

Krickeberg, Walter, *Märchen der Azteken und Inkaperuaner, Maya und* Muisca übersetz eingeleites und erlautert, Jena, 1928.

Mérida, Carlos, *Estampas del Popol Vuh,* Mexico, 1943.

Memorial of *Tecpan Atitlan,* Spanish translation by Juan Gavarrete Guatemala, 1873-74.

Morley, Sylvanus Griswold, *The Ancient Maya,* Stanford Univ., Calif., 1946.

Muller, Friedrich Max, *Chips from a German Workshop,* London, 1867.

Pohorilles, Noah Ellieser. *Das Popol Vuh, Die mystische Geschischte des Kice-Volkes von Guatemala nach dem Original-Texte übersetz und heartheitet.* Leipzig, 1913.

Raynaud, Georges, *Les Manuscrits Précolombiens,* Paris, 1893.

————, *Les dieux, les héros et les hommes d l'ancient Guatémala d'apres le Livre du Conseil (Popol Vuh),* Paris, 1925.

Recinos, Adrián, *Popol Vuh. Las historias antiguas del Quiché,* Translation from the original Quiché text. Mexico, 1947.

————, *Memorial de Sololá, Anales de los Cakchiqueles.* Translation from the original manuscript, Mexico, 1950.

Rodas N., Flavio, *Simbolismos de Guatemala*. Guatemala, 1938.

Roys, R. L., *The Ethno-Botany of the Maya,* New Orleans, 1931.

Scherzer, Karl von, *Mitteilungen über die Handschriftlichen Werke des* Padre Francisco Ximenez in der Universitäts-Bibliothek zu Guatemala, Vienna, 1856.

Schuller, Rudolph, *Der Verfasser des Popol Vuh. Anthropos.* Vol., XXVI, Nos. 5-6. Vienna ,1931.

Schultze Jena, Leonhard, *Leben, Glaube und Sprache des Quiche von Guatemala.* Indiana I. Jena, 1933.

Seler, Eduard, *Der Bedeutungswandel in den Mythen des Popol Vuh. Eine Kritik."* In Athropos. Vol., VIII, 1904.

Spence, Lewis, *The Popol Vuh.* The Mythic and Heroic Sagas of the Kiches of Central America. London, 1908.

————, *The Popol Vuh: America's oldest book.* The Open Court Vol., XI, II, Chicago, 1928.

Villacorta, C. J. Antonio, *Prehistoria a Historia Antigua de Guatemala,* Guatemala, 1938.

Villacorta C, J. A. and Flavio Rodas, *Manuscrito de Chichicastenango.* El Popol Vuh. Quiché text and Spanish translation, Guatemala, 1927.

Vocabulario de las Lenguas Quiché y Kakchiquel, Manuscript in the American Collection of Brasseur de Bourbourg. No. 65. Bibliotheque Nationale, Paris.

Ximenez, Fr. Francisco, *Las Historias del Origen de los Indios de esta Provincia de Guatemala* . . . etc. First translation into Spanish from Quiche text, and published for the first time by Dr. C. Scherzer, Vienna.

————, *Historia de la Provincia de San Vicente de Chiapas y Guatemala.* Ed. Sociedad de Geografia e Historia. Guatemala, 1929-31.

————, *Arte de las tres lenguas:* Cacchiquel, Quiché y Tzutuhil Manuscript, Newberry Library, Chicago.

————, *Historia Natural del Rejno de Guatemala.* Manuscript. Sociedad de Geografia e Historia. Guatemala.

Zorita, Alonso, *Breve y Sumaria Relación de los Señores de la Nueva España.* Nueva colección de documentos para la historia de México. Vol., III. Mexico, 1892.

————, *Historia de la Nueva España.* Colección de libros y documentos referentes a la Historia de América, Madrid, 1909.

DATE DUE

OCT 5 '70			